TARGET - DRESDEN

By

Alan W Cooper

Published in 1995 by
Independent Books
3 Leaves Green Crescent
Keston
Bromley BR2 6DN
GREAT BRITAIN

Edited by David Tindall

ISBN 1-872836-15-1

A catalogue record for this book is available from the British Library

Printed and bound in Great Britain by Bookcraft (Bath) Ltd.

CONTENTS

PHOTOGRAPHS AND ILLUSTRATIONS

SOURCES

The Origins of Strategic Bombing	Neville Jones
The Zeppelin Fighters	Arch Whitehouse
RFC - A History	Geoffrey Norris
Dresden 1945	Alexander McKee
The Right of Line	John Terraine
Bombers Battle	Wing Commander Saunders
Dresden im Luftkrieg	Gotz Bergander
The Bombing of Germany	Hans Rumapt
Doodlebugs and Rockets	Bob Ogley
Most Secret War	Dr R V Jones
They Saved London	Bernard Newman
The War in the Air	H A Jones
The Destruction of Dresden	David Irving
Goebbels War Diaries	Hugh Trevor -Roper
The German Air Force	Asher Lee
Bomber Harris	Dudley Saward
Bomber Offensive	Sir Arthur Harris
Battle of the Ruhr	Alan Cooper
Bombers Over Berlin	Alan Cooper
Beyond the Dams to the Tirpitz	Alan Cooper
The Struggle for Europe	Chester Wilmot
Inside the Third Reich	Albert Speer
Bomber Command War Diaries	Middlebrook/ Everitt
Blockade by Air	J. M Spaight
The Offensive Weapon	David Wragg
Wings Over Gloucester	John Rennison
The Three Star Blitz	Charles Whitting

TARGET - DRESDEN

INTRODUCTION

For the crews of Bomber Command the war was fought many miles away, deep in the heart of enemy territory, or enemy occupied territory. The battle started on the first day of war, in September 1939, and did not end until April 1945. Night after night, and later by day, they went out into combat, showing, time after time, the highest dedication and courage, most of which went unseen in the black skies of night.

Following Dunkirk, Bomber Command was the only force which remained on the offensive and took the fight to the enemy. Its presence over Europe night after night let the resistance fighters know that Great Britain had not been invaded, as the German propaganda machine wanted them to believe, and that it was worth fighting on.

The role of Bomber Command in World War II was an important one and history shows that it contributed greatly to the winning of the war in Europe. The intensive interrogation of a number of German senior officers at the end of the war endorsed this fact. Among the targets listed to be attacked were cities and towns. One such target was the city of Dresden, deep into enemy territory.

'The Luftwaffe was finished'; '... an undefended city that was not contributing to the war effort and therefore didn't warrant the attack.'

These were some of the things said after the raid in February 1945, and repeated over the intervening years. Arguably these statements are speculative, but the fact is that, between the Dresden raid and the end of the war, over 300 Allied aircraft were lost, mainly to *Luftwaffe* nightfighters. The Germans had the jet engine and their advanced fighters were still very much in evidence in the skies over Germany. They had developed both the VI and V2 and were experimenting with an inter-continental version of the A2 rocket. The best intelligence showed that they were well advanced in their atomic research and that, coupled with the delivery system available in their rockets, was a terrifying prospect. It is easier, with the benefit of hindsight, to place the Dresden raid near to the end of the war, but in 1945 there was no timescale, only the experience of five years of unremitting war.

Similarly, the charge is that the RAF deliberately produced a firestorm in Dresden like that which had razed Hamburg. Again this is speculative, since a firestorm depends upon almost freak meteorological conditions and in particular hinges on the adiabatic lapse rate. Those conditions prevailed in Hamburg on the night of the terrible fires and came together again on the night of the raid on Dresden. If it is proof of guilt to suggest that sufficient incendiaries were dropped to start a firestorm, then the charge is proven; but similar amounts had been dropped on numerous other targets throughout the war without the same result.

What is clear is that those aircrew who undertook the long flight to Dresden on that February night were carrying out their duty in the face of well established odds. Many were at the end of tours of operations, while others were screwing up their courage for one of their first. Either way, they were young men fighting for what they believed was right. Not monsters or *'Terrorflieger'(sic)*. If there is guilt to be shouldered for the unbelievable carnage that was Dresden, then it rests with the politicians - not with those who were tasked with its execution.

The wartime cost to Bomber Command was extremely high: over 56,000 men died in action or in training for operations. Only 13 out of every 100 men who served as aircrew in Bomber Command survived.

In 1943, at the height of the bomber offensive, 1,000 men were required each month to replace those who failed to return and sustain the offensive. Many of the men killed are buried in cemeteries all over Europe, but for those 20,000 who have no known graves there is the Runnymede Memorial. There, along with their names, is the simple inscription:

'I gave my today for your tomorrow.'

All over East Anglia, Lincolnshire and Yorkshire are the ghosts of bomber crews who failed to return to base or crashed on take off, or on landing. Some of the airfields, such as RAF Scampton, are still active and others, like East Kirkby and Elvington, have been partly refurbished as a living memorial to those men. But many have reverted back to farm land and the efforts of the men who served there are largely forgotten, though not by all.

I, for one, salute the tremendous courage, dedication and skill of those crews and, wherever they are today, may their landings be safe ones.

Alan W Cooper, Gloucester, 1995

ABBREVIATIONS:

AC	- Aircraftman
AI	- Air Interception (Airborne Radar)
AOC	- Air Officer Commanding
AP	- Aiming Point
BA	- Blind Approach
C in C	- Commander in Chief
Cpl	- Corporal
EA	- Enemy Aircraft
GCI	- Ground Controlled Interception
HE	- High Explosive
HQ	- Headquarters
IFF	- Identification Friend (or) Foe
KG	- *Kampfgeschwader* - Bomber Wing - *Luftwaffe*
LAC	- Leading Aircraftman
MT	- Motor Transport
OTU	- Operational Training Unit
P/O	- Pilot Officer
PRU	- Photographic Reconnaissance Unit
Sgt	- Sergeant
S/L	- Squadron Leader
TI	- Target Indicator
VHF	- Very High Frequency
Wg Cdr	- Wing Commander

CHAPTER ONE

AERIAL WARFARE

One of many new forms of warfare appeared in World War I and has been used to increasing effect ever since. Along with the introduction of machine guns, tanks and U-Boats came the use of the aeroplane. The employment of aeroplanes in land and sea battles instituted a change of fundamental importance: whereas the operations of the belligerents had previously been confined to the land and sea, now the whole of the sky had become a combat area. In the past, battles were only conflicts of armies and navies of individual states. People and dynasties were only concerned indirectly with them.

In the future, the difference would be the process and development of technology. Victory would come from the people who could destroy the material and moral reserves of the enemy. With the advent of an air arm the whole territory of nations came within the scope of the attacking weapons of the enemy, and could become a theatre of war as well as the battlefield. The victory would fall to that side which was able to destroy the resistance of the enemy, both materially and morally. The main burden of the battle in future wars would be borne by the air force, with attacks on the enemy's sources of power. It was the opinion of historians that this would be the most effective form of warfare.

However, attacks from the air would be the most difficult in terms of accuracy and, of course, the early flying machines were extremely vulnerable to attack and mechanical failure. A flying force would be used offensively as well as for defence. When the air force could be used to maximum efficiency, the total effectiveness of the armed forces would reach its zenith: the army could operate on land and the navy at sea, whilst the air force could combine with both and also take on independent operations. The ability of an air force to hit and cripple the heart of an enemy nation at the outset of hostilities was a tactic waiting to be tested.

Opinion was that war in the air would never present a scenario where two opposing air forces were actively in combat, rather than acting as a support arm for one of the two 'senior' services. Little did military thinking realise that, within a few years, a whole campaign would hinge on the outcome of an air battle.

On both sides, attacks against enemy territory would start in order to strike at the centre of resistance. The first targets would be static objects, the ground organisation of the enemy air force and its aircraft industry. In executing such attacks, the stronger side would not need to avoid air combat, but the weaker side would have to do so. The bomber was advocated to be the basic type of the air force of the future, in order to possess a comparatively stable fighting force in the air. An *'air cruiser'* would combine the qualities of a bomber with heavy armament and strong construction. An air battle would be carried out, although it was regarded as an important advantage if it could be conducted with a compact group of aircraft of similar types. There were two vital factors to consider:

1. Was supremacy in the air really of such great importance?

2. Could supremacy be attained ?

From direct air attack on the enemy front it was expected that considerable damage to morale and material could be achieved.

The overwhelming importance of the air force lay in the wide scope of its operational actions. The choice of targets was dependent upon a series of considerations of military, political, social and psychological significance.

The first bombs to fall from an aeroplane were dropped in 1911 by the Italians. This (then illegal) act took place during the Italian - Turkish war. Lieutenant Gavotti carried four bombs in a leather bag and dropped one from 600 feet on a Turkish encampment: he was so excited by the results that he then dropped the remainder in a second run on the target. Such weapons were, in those days, more like grenades than bombs and weighed about four and half pounds.

In 1916, Trenchard said:

> 'The aeroplane is not a defence against the aeroplane. But the opinion of those more competent to judge is that the aeroplane, as a weapon of attack, cannot be too highly estimated.'

In 1913, bombing experiments were carried out, from which it was concluded that an aeroplane dropping a 100lb bomb, containing 40lb of explosive from a height of 350 feet, could not itself be endangered from the resulting explosion. Strategic bombing was meant to weaken the enemy's resources so that eventually he would have to fight his battle virtually unarmed; also to attack communications other than the immediate communications of an army in the field, and to attack airfield factories, but not airfields. Most especially it would apply to all attacks on the enemy's industries. It would be at long range, which was the purpose of a main bomber force.

In 1909, Lord Montagu of Beaulieu, at a meeting of the National Defence Association, outlined the effects of a raid on London by a fleet of airships - attacks directed against the *'nerve centre'* of the capital, on targets such as the Houses of Parliament, Government Offices and telephone exchanges, which could paralyse the nation.

He was implicit that, in future wars, the enemy would not hesitate to use air bombardment to achieve a possible victory; and that London would be a prominent target.

In 1912, a German naval officer in Kiel gave a lecture on bombing from the air. He said that the bombing of England would cause serious material damage and also affect the morale of the people. So the air war on England was being considered and planned two years before the war actually began. The signs were there in 1910 that Great Britain would be subject to attack from the air in a future war. Had Germany decided to begin a bombing campaign at the onset of WWI, she could have done so with complete impunity.

In 1912, the subject was considered again, and steps were taken to defend London with guns and searchlights. The Admiralty met to decide how to protect vital targets from aerial attack, which they knew the Hague Convention would not prevent. The First Sea Lord, Winston Churchill, suggested blackout precautions being introduced. In Germany, Zeppelin airships were being armed with machine guns and bomb compartments. This could only mean one thing in the event of a future war.

Captains Fulton and Dickson were inspired, by French achievements, to learn flying at their own expense, and both afterwards laboured to convert others to a belief in its value. A memorandum by Dickson in 1912 showed how keenly he was alive to possible trends in the future:

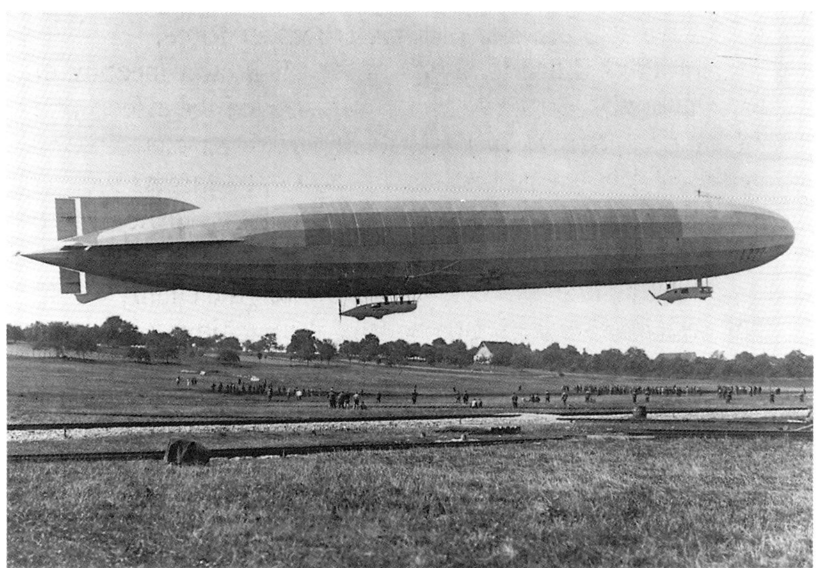

German Military Airship LZ.77. Completed Friedrichshafen, commissioned 24th August 1915. Capacity 1,126,700 cu. ft. Length 536.4 ft, diameter 61.35 ft. Powered by four 240 hp Maybach engines. Speed 61 mph, ceiling 12,800 ft. This airship carried out raids over Essex on 11th September 1915 (Hauptmann Horn commanding). Brought down by gun fire Revigny, France, 21st February 1916.

'In the case of a European war between two countries, both sides would be equipped with large corps of aeroplanes, each trying to obtain information about the other, and to hide its own movements. The efforts which each would exert, in order to hinder or prevent the enemy from obtaining information, would lead to the inevitable result of a war in the air, for the supremacy of the air, by armed aeroplanes operating against each other. This fight for the

> supremacy of the air in future wars will be of the first and greatest importance, and when it has been won, the land and sea forces of the loser will be at such a disadvantage that the war will certainly have to terminate at a much smaller loss in men and money to both sides.'

The writing was on the wall, as it were, but who would read it?

CHAPTER TWO

WORLD WAR ONE

In 1899, the Germans, flying the lighter type airships, began dropping bombs from these machines. When World War I began in 1914, Germany had a fleet of six Zeppelin airships, and it seemed obvious to many that these would eventually be used to attack Great Britain.

On 26th August 1914, it was reported that the Zeppelins had bombed Antwerp, dropping six bombs at night and killing 12 civilians. A hospital was damaged, despite the fact that it was flying the flag of the Geneva Convention at the time. The bombs were reported to have exploded with 'terrific force.'

Damage to Albert Street, King's Lynn, 1915
(Imperial War Museum)

When war with Great Britain was declared in September 1914, Captain Peter Strasser and Dr Hugo Eckener had become the aerial warlords in Germany. They wanted to start attacks on the UK straightaway, but the Kaiser was opposed to them. A year was to pass before he gave permission for attacks to commence and, even then, there were strict conditions: no deliberate attacks were to be made on Buckingham Palace, St Paul's Cathedral, Westminster Abbey, or Government Buildings. There were no restrictions about bombing hospitals, schools, or civilian homes.

In November 1914, Admiral Alfred von Tirpitz, the German Secretary of State for the German Navy, said:

> 'The English are now in terror of the Zeppelins, perhaps not without reason. I contend here for the standpoint of 'an eye for an eye' but I am not in favour of 'frightfulness'. Also, the indiscriminate dropping of bombs is wrong; they are repulsive when they hit and kill old women and one gets used to them. If one could set a line to London in thirty places then the repulsiveness would be lost sight of in the immensity of the effect.'

As was to be the case twenty-five years later, the Germans did not commence bombing the British mainland until the second year of the war. The first raid on the UK took place on 19/20th January 1915, when two airships bombed Sheringham, Snettisham, Thornham, Brancaster, King's Lynn and Yarmouth in East Anglia. Four people were killed and sixteen injured, of whom fifteen were civilians. In future any man, woman, or child in a country at war could expect to be attacked at any time - the air war against civilians had begun. The Zeppelins would return and attack the UK on nineteen further occasions in 1915.

As well as the Zeppelins, there were attacks by seaplanes. On 21st February 1915, incendiary bombs were dropped by seaplanes in the areas of Clacton and Colchester Barracks: one bomb hit a house, but no lives were lost on this occasion. The first attack on London took place on 31st May 1915, when 25 high explosives and 87 incendiaries were dropped from Zeppelin L.38 on Stoke Newington, Hoxton, Shoreditch, Whitechapel, Stepney, West Ham and Leytonstone. Seven people were killed and 35 injured, 33 being civilians. Two of those killed had their clothes burned off in the explosion. This was the first of 52 raids on London by Zeppelin airships.

On 17th August 1915, L.10 reached London and bombed Leytonstone and Wanstead Flats: ten people were killed and 48 injured. On 8th September 1915, 22 people were killed and 87 injured when L.13 dropped bombs with some effect, leaving in its wake fire and destruction across Euston, Theobalds Road, Gray's Inn Road and down to Liverpool Street. Fifteen high explosives and 55 incendiary bombs were dropped. On 13th October 1915 came another severe raid in which casualties were high. Eighty one bombs fell on London out of a total of 189 dropped, the remainder falling over East Anglia en route to London: one fell in front of the Lyceum Theatre, killing 17 people and injuring 21. Near the Strand Theatre four were killed and 15 injured. Total casualties were 71 killed and 128 injured, of whom 47 were killed and 102 injured in London. Up to January 1916, twenty-one raids had been made, 1,900 bombs dropped, 277 people killed and 645 others injured.

On 2nd September 1916, 463 bombs were dropped - 4 people were killed and 12 injured. It was on this raid that Lieutenant William Leefe-Robinson shot down L.11, for which achievement he was later awarded the Victoria

Cross.

On 23rd September 1916 came another heavy raid: 371 bombs were dropped in Mitcham, Streatham, Brixton, Kennington, Lea Bridge Road and Leyton. With casualties in Yorkshire, Norfolk, Lincolnshire and Essex added to those for London, 40 people were killed and 130 injured on this one day.

Air raid damage. Chancery Lane, London, W.C.
Airship raid of 13/14th October 1915.
(Imperial War Museum)

The first aeroplane attack on London was on the night of 28th November 1916, when six high explosive bombs of small size were dropped by one aircraft, an LVG CII Armed Reconnaissance machine, in the area of the Victoria Palace Music Hall, opposite Victoria Station. The bomb dropped on the roof and destroyed part of the dressing room area, wounding one woman. In all, four men and five women were slightly injured, the most serious case being the woman injured at the Music Hall. The aircraft also took twenty photographs of a number of military installations en route to London, but had to turn back through engine trouble to force land in Boulogne, where it was captured.

The first daylight aeroplane raid on the UK came on 25th May 1917, when 23 Gotha aircraft, led by *Hauptmann* Ernst Brandenberg, set out for London but only got as far as Gravesend. There they turned back because of cloud, but as they did so they dropped bombs on Shorncliffe Camp and on Cheriton: 95 people were killed and 195 injured. The majority of the casualties were in the crowded thoroughfare near the harbour, where people had congregated to do their Whitsun shopping.

In Germany, General Ludendorff, in his *'Kriegfuhrung und Politik'* (Conduct of War and Politics), writing on the position in the Spring of 1917, shortly before the commencement of air raids on Great Britain by *Bombengeschwader 3*, said:

'In the meantime it has become a matter of urgent necessity to supplement by extensive propaganda on a large scale the purely military warfare and the economic warfare which set in with the unrestricted submarine action and making war on the morale of the enemy peoples and armies. The plan is to ensure the final victory by sowing dissension among the Allies and taking from them their faith in ultimate victory.'

Gotha G.5 fitted with two 260 hp Mercedes engines. (Imperial War Museum)

The air raids on Great Britain were specially designed to carry this plan into effect. During a period of German military successes and serious depression amongst the Allies, the timely and intensive employment of bombing squadrons in raids on London might have been a decisive factor in the whole trend of the war. Led up to by the Zeppelin raids, war was, for the first time in military history, to be carried beyond the actual theatre of war to the capital of the enemy country, the nerve centre of the nation, the centre of resistance and the source of supplies. The main object was the moral intimidation of the British nation, then crippling of the will to fight, thus preparing the ground for peace. These ends achieved, the British Government might fall, 'the solidarity of the enemy nations' be shaken and the bombing squadron would have contributed an important part towards the attainment of the final victory.

The secondary objectives in view were the crippling of the British war supplies industry, of communications between the coast and London, of the coastal depots and of transport across the English Channel. The main objective of the raids was London, the heart of the British nation, the base of operations of the Entente and all the Allied and Associated Powers, the centre for the conduct of the war and of the war industry. In London itself the main objectives were the Government buildings around Downing Street, the Admiralty, the Bank of England and the Press buildings in Fleet Street. The coastal towns between Harwich and Folkestone and the localities on the way to London were to serve as secondary objectives when it was impossible, on account of the weather, or for technical reasons, to reach London.

The most experienced German pilots were formed into a unit which was originally called the 'Ostend Carrier-Pigeon Squadron', and now became *Englandgeschwader* (Bombing Squadron No 3), their task being to bomb London.

The first daylight raid on London was on 13th June 1917, when 14 Gotha bombers reached London at 11.30am and 118 bombs were dropped around Liverpool Street Station. Casualties amounted to 162 people killed and 432 injured, the highest casualties in one raid since WWI had started. All but 11 casualties were civilians, including 43 children who were pupils of Upper North Street School in Poplar. A 50 kg bomb passed through the roof and three floors of the school to the ground floor. In its passage 2 children were killed, and half the bomb was torn away: the remainder, however, exploded among 64 children, killing 16 and injuring 30, along with 2 men and 2 women. Another school had a narrow escape when a bomb passed through five floors but failed to explode.

The Mayor of Poplar stated that, from all he had seen and heard, the British were a nation of lions governed by asses. The industrial unrest was imputed by the Commission of Enquiry to various causes, but it seemed to be forgotten that many thousands of munitions workers were dissatisfied because there was no protection available for their wives and children.

As a direct reaction, on 15th June, a cry went up for Berlin to be bombed by 500 aeroplanes, and for the enemy to be 'paid back in kind'.

On 27th June 1917, an expert writing in 'Aeroplane' magazine recommended, as an answer to the German air raids, '... extensive bombing of the iron mines, gun factories and all armament factories behind the German front, destroying the sources of power to paralyse German resistance at the front and create unemployment.' The newspapers went on to record in some detail the British raids on the Ruhr, such as at Essen, which were very much exaggerated to pacify public opinion regarding casualties and damage in the Britain.

The General Post Office in London, following aeroplane raid of 7th July 1917. (Imperial War Museum)

Pancras Road, King's Cross. Daylight aeroplane raid of 7th July 1917 (Imperial War Museum).

In 'The Times' newspaper the Bishops of Oxford and Ely stated that they were against reprisals which they considered wrong and immoral.

On 7th July 1917, 53 people were killed and 182 injured when bombs were dropped on Margate and in the City and East End of London. This was the last time London was attacked by day in WWI.

On 11th July 1917, the War Cabinet agreed to a Committee on Air Organisation and Home Defence against Air Raids being formed under the Prime Minister, Lloyd George: Lord Montagu of Beaulieu seemed to think the Germans had the right to bomb London, saying that it was defended by guns and aeroplanes and was the chief centre for the production of munitions (Woolwich Arsenal). He predicted that air attacks would be nerve-shattering to people rather than a threat on sea or land. He also said that Britain was behind other continental air powers, and urged that an adequate air force for defence be formed.

The newspapers were stirring things up too. An article in 'The Globe' said: 'The next big raid may cost 5,000 people their lives instead of the 500 on this occasion and may lead to a revolt and the fall of the Government.' 'The Daily Mail' said: 'As far as aeroplane construction is concerned, the enemy has the upper hand. All those responsible for this should be dismissed. There will be no improvement until we have an Air Ministry.' 'The Times' of 24th July 1917 published an article by the President of the 'Londoners' League' in which he stated that the lessons of this war (meaning the air raids on London) could not be forgotten. In the future there would be no place for any German in Great Britain.

General Jan Smuts who, in 1917, was in Britain from South Africa as a member of the War Cabinet, was asked to investigate the problems of 'Air organisations and the direction of aerial operations.' He recorded in his report of

August 1917 that '...air power can be used as an independent means of war operations. Nobody who witnessed the attacks on London on 17th July,' he added, 'could have any doubt on that point.'

General Smuts' report, now thought of as perhaps the most important paper in the history of the creation of the Royal Air Force, made a number of very relevant points: aeroplanes being used for independent operations - the day would come, he speculated, when air operations would be undertaken in enemy airspace and the destruction of industrial centres and concentrations of population on a vast scale might become the principle operation of war, making the older forms of military and naval operations secondary and subordinate. As soon as his report was accepted by the Government of the day, the Air Board called upon a number of experts to advise on the formulation of a bombing policy.

Among the first called in was Lord Tiverton, serving with the naval section of the British Aviation Commission in Paris.

He had made a detailed study of strategic bombing, his object to discover what knowledge and skills were essential to success in this type of bombing. He was requested to submit to the Board a paper on bombing covering any point he thought relevant. In his paper dated 3rd September 1917, he first dealt with targets and drew up a list of possible objectives, dividing them geographically into four groups.

The first three were the industrial areas around the cities of Dusseldorf, Cologne and Mannheim: the fourth was the steel industry of the Saar Valley. Day or night bombing was another point he considered. His preference was day bombing because:

> 'The greatest moral effect is by day when the operatives are actively engaged in their work or in the streets without any particular place to go to, rather than by night when they are in their own houses where they have at any rate got a roof over their heads, a fact which gives a considerable practical factor of safety against stray shells from anti-aircraft fire.'

Periods of good weather and moonlight were two of the factors against night bombing, in Tiverton's opinion. The first of what, some years later, would be called 'The Blitz' started on 24th September 1917, leaving 21 dead and 70 injured.

The Danish newspaper 'Berlingske Tindende' stated on 26th September 1917:

> 'The German air raid on the night of 24th September 1917 was undoubtedly the longest and most intense so far experienced by London. It lasted over an hour and the bombing was very heavy at times. The airmen evidently flew very high as it was impossible to see them, whilst the British aeroplanes could plainly be seen. The reports published up to the present show that the Germans were not specially successful. The British public is once more clamouring for British airmen to carry out reprisal raids on German towns.'

On the 25th, 9 were killed and 23 injured, followed on the 29th by 14 killed and 87 injured.

After four raids in a week 300,000 people in London were using the Underground stations as shelters from the air attacks. The general opinion was that something had to be done and that counter measures should be taken against the German raids on the UK, such as:

1. A joint military and naval action to drive the Germans back from the coast of Flanders.

2. An air offensive against the German air bases in Flanders.

A raid on 19th October 1917, in which bombs were dropped on Lewisham, Piccadilly and Camberwell, left 33 dead and 49 injured. One bomb that fell in Piccadilly Circus opposite Swan and Edgar's was responsible for many of the casualties.

In October 1917, Winston Churchill wrote:

> 'It is improbable that any terrorisation of the civil population which could be achieved by air attack could compel the government of a great nation to surrender. Familiarity with bombardment, a good system of dugouts or shelters, and a strong control by police and military authorities, would be sufficient to preserve the national fighting power unimpaired. In our own case we have seen the combative spirit of the people roused, and not quelled, by the German air raids...'

On November 22nd, Tiverton put forward his second paper on bombing: this was entirely devoted to targets and their selection. As a basis for his work he assumed that, of 2,000 aircraft in a bomber force, which was the figure he was instructed to use in his first paper, 1,000 would be available at any time to attack a specific target. Making allowance for bombing errors, he calculated, among other things, the probable numbers of bombs (a) likely to fall within the factory area and (b) likely to cause effective damage. Large factories, he considered, were easy to hit but difficult to destroy; small factories were easy to destroy but difficult to hit.

On 15th December 1917 Lord Robertson, speaking in London during the discussion of the work of the Air Board, stated that reprisal air raids were being planned and said:

> 'It is our duty to avenge the murder of innocent women and children. If the enemy will not change his tactics, the saying 'a tooth for a tooth' will be fulfilled. In this matter we are for full and entirely satisfactory reprisals. General Ludendorff stated that this war is a war of nations and gave us to understand that the civilian population might fall victims of the airmen's bombs, just as much as the armies in the field. We abhor this point of view and consider it absolutely immoral. But in a struggle for our existence and for the lives of our women and children we cannot allow a one-sided application. We cannot allow the wily enemy any further advantage. We are firmly resolved to avenge every attack on the life of the civil population of this country in a like manner.'

December 18 saw the last raid of 1917 by 15 Gothas and 1 'Giant'[1] aeroplane: one of the bombs dropped was 300 kg, the largest so far dropped from an enemy aircraft on Britain. One bomb fell in the gardens of Buckingham Palace. In this raid 13 people were killed and 79 injured.

On 28/29th January 1918, a large area of London was attacked by 4 Giant aircraft, dropping 44 bombs which killed 65 people and injured 159.

Odhams Printing Works, 93, Long Acre, London, W.C. following aeroplane raid of 29/29 January 1918. View of the collapsed portion of the building. The casualties occurred in the basement where the men seen in the photograph are standing, and around the printing machines in the foreground. (Imperial War Museum)

On 16th February 1918, two Giant aircraft reached London and one dropped a bomb on the Chelsea Hospital, killing 5 people. The second bombed Woolwich and Beckenham, killing 7 people and injuring 2. The Woolwich bomb was the first one-ton bomb dropped in WWI, but not the last dropped by *Reisenflugzeugabteilung* 501 before the war was to end, nine months later.

Air Raid damage to Chelsea Hospital, 16th February 1918.
(Imperial War Museum)

On March 18th 1918, the 'Daily Mail' offered the following in its editorial:

> 'It would be a great mistake for the allies to come to any agreement regarding the war in the air which would prevent them making the fullest use of their air supremacy.'

The attitude of the British Nation was well portrayed in a letter found on a dead British soldier dated 4th March 1918. Part of it read:

> 'In a sense these air raids are good for us, they shake us up and do relatively little damage, considering the size of London. The Germans are stupid, because the air raids only bring out the best in Britain, money is forthcoming, all the men will join up and England will find it the more difficult to forget since practically only the women and children are killed.'

Smuts advocated all air services being amalgamated, and on 1st April 1918, the Royal Flying Corps and the Royal Naval Air Service merged to become the new Royal Air Force.

On 19/20th May 1918 came the last attack at night, when 43 Gothas took off to attack London: only 13 reached their target since the defences (guns which fired some 3,000 shells, and 84 night fighters) managed to account for 6 of the enemy aircraft. A seventh crashed with engine trouble at Clacton and the eighth came to grief in Belgium. Despite these relatively powerful defences 49 people were killed and 177 injured in the attack. The Germans never came again in WWI, the first *'Battle of Britain'* was over and the first serious confrontation between bombers and fighters had taken place.

In 8 daylight and 19 night raids by the Gothas 435 people had been killed and 997 injured. In all, between 1914 and 1918, there had been 103 raids by airship and aeroplane, dropping over 8,000 bombs, killing 1,414 people and injuring 3,416. Of this total 670 had been killed in London and 1,960 injured. The Gotha and Giant raids had accounted for 60% of the casualties. In Great Britain the defences were 469 anti-aircraft guns, 622 searchlights, 259 height finders and 10 sound locators, in all manned by 6,136 officers and men.

In May 1918 the time had come, in the opinion of the Air Council, to form an Independent Force for large scale bombing attacks on Germany. In the Britain the idea of bombing had made little progress. However, in 1917, a paper had been prepared at Trenchard's HQ entitled 'Long Distance Bombing.' In it Trenchard expressed his view that morale was as important, if not more important, than material damage.

In 1917, a special unit had been formed in the UK known as the 8th Brigade, consisting of DH 4 day bombers, FE2B's, and Handley Page night bombers. On 5th June 1918, after 142 operations, the original 8th Brigade Squadrons were joined by a force known as the Independent Force, under Major-General Hugh Trenchard. Its role was to mount an offensive against German industries and, in the last few months of WWI, a number of attacks on German industrial towns on the Rhine were made. Five hundred and fifty tons of bombs were dropped with a noticeable reduction in German production and, to some degree, in the morale of the German people.

Some 210 targets were listed in Germany and France. It was advocated that long distance bombing would produce the maximum morale effect only if the visits were constantly repeated at short intervals, so as to produce, in each area bombed, sustained anxiety. The Super Handley Page bombers were capable of carrying 230 lb bombs and were to be used in attacks on Berlin. Fortunately (or unfortunately) attacks by these bombers did not materialise, as the Armistice came in November 1918 and with it the end of the war.

In 1921, the Italian General Guillio Douhet published a paper entitled: 'The Theory of Air War in the Future'.

The first essentials suggested were:

> 'To eliminate the enemy air force's operations by attacks on the opposing ground organisations, and the destruction of enemy flying units in the air.'

Douhet was an artillery officer, and later qualified for the General Staff and Command of the Airship Battalions. In 1915, he produced a report criticising the Italian methods of conducting war, was court martialled, found guilty and sentenced to a year's imprisonment. After his report was vindicated, his sentence was quashed and he was released from prison and reinstated to his position in the army. In 1921, he was promoted to General and devoted himself to the science of warfare. He was of the opinion that a war would last only one month if the most important of the large towns, and centres of industry and commerce, could be attacked with 300 tons of bombs. He also considered that the obliteration of these towns would mean a complete breakdown of the basic social system of a nation. He suggested the creation of a unified Ministry of Defence and High Command and postulated two main aims of the armed forces:

1. Defence of the Homeland.

2. Attacks on enemy defensive positions in order to penetrate enemy territory.

For air defence, he considered that the only solution was anti-aircraft fire which could be concentrated around the most important objectives. Air attacks would start in order to strike at the centre of resistance. The first targets would be static, such as the ground organisation of the enemy air force and its aircraft industry. It was basically a matter of indifference to Douhet whether the war was on land, at sea or in the air, although he recognised the sky as the main battle area.

In 1981, 'Bomber' Harris said, when interviewed:

> 'In the First World War there was a casualty known as shell shock, fellows who were knocked stupid by the effect of a nearby explosion, and the nearest thing that was ever likely to explode near them, except for a few mines, was a five-inch shell. It contained, honestly, a handful of explosive, and the smallest thing we used in World War Two was a 1,000lb bomb containing 200 or 300 lbs of explosives two or three times as effective, pound for pound, as the explosives of the First War.'

Out of the First World War, and the use of bomber aircraft, arose the new concept of the vulnerability of civilians. Bomber aircraft, in attempting to bomb military and industrial targets in poor weather conditions, had begun the bombing of the civilian population and the proposition that civilian morale could break under heavy air attacks had come to the fore.

When WWI ended, in 1918, the RAF had the largest air force in the world consisting of 300 Squadrons which comprised 233,000 officers and men, 23,000 aircraft and 700 airfields; but by 1921 only 21 Squadrons remained. The attitude of the Army and Navy was that the RAF was of little use in war other than for reconnaissance and artillery spotting for the Army.

---

[1] - *'Giant' - the popular name for the huge aircraft built by Zeppelin-Staaken. The last Mark of this truly vast aeroplane, the RXI, had a wingspan of 138 feet (larger than the Avro Lancaster of WW II), a length of 73 feet 10 inches and stood some 20 ft from the ground at the cockpit. It weighed 22,780 lbs empty (31,790 lbs fully laden) and was capable of a sedate 81.25 mph. Armed with five machine guns this lumbering giant could climb to 9,800 feet in seventy minutes!*

CHAPTER THREE

BETWEEN THE WARS

The Treaty of Versailles, signed in June 1919, stipulated that the Germans were no longer to maintain anything but minimal army or naval forces, and that the air force be disbanded. As a direct result over 15,000 aircraft and more than 25,000 aero engines were handed over to the Allies. Civilian aircraft would be permitted but, in 1922, a limitation was imposed on their size.

In the United Kingdom, the Navy and the Army argued against aircraft becoming an integral part of the older services, and were bitterly opposed to the RAF becoming a third and equal service. However, Trenchard, the first Chief of the Air Staff, weathered the storm, and the Government held enquiries into proposals for a division in the air services, but each time re-affirmed its determination to maintain a separate Air Force: nevertheless, by 1921, the 1918 inventory of 300 Squadrons had been reduced to just 24.

The Air Staff estimated that in a future war, bombing casualties would be 50 per ton of explosives dropped on Britain. As they saw it, the Gotha and 'Giant' night raids had inflicted casualties at the rate of 52 per ton. The bomber force must be maintained and, in theory, at a greater strength than the enemy could manage. The only defence lay in aggressive counter-attack; the only hope of victory in deploying a more powerful bomber force. Although the resulting force was not as powerful as had been hoped, had it been any less so it would not have been possible to form the RAF in 1918. Nor would it have been possible, in the war that was to come twenty years later, to field a credible bomber force. The Air Staff saw clearly that the bomb was the offensive weapon of the Air Force: the fighter would be needed to deal with enemy bombers. Thus it was decided that the new Air Defence of Great Britain should have bomber and fighter squadrons in the ratio of two-thirds bombers to one-third fighters. It was Squadron Leader Arthur Harris's opinion that bombing was the main task of the RAF, but that it could not be used in the correct way under the control of the army in combined operations. Harris, at the time, was commanding 45 Squadron.

In 1922, in Iraq and Transjordan, a small air force was formed, and a very successful system, known as the 'air control of underdeveloped countries', was instituted. It did not mount direct attacks on the tribesmen or their houses, but was a form of blockade. Unlike a sea blockade, aimed at the slow strangulation of a country, these air attacks were designed for discomfort and inconvenience. (This system proved so economical that it was later, in 1928, extended to Aden.)

In Iraq, in 1923, Harris developed the prone position for the bomb-aimer to obtain a good view of the target.

The Tribesmen who raided other villages were ordered to surrender themselves for trial in a court of law. When they refused, warning leaflets were dropped from the air, telling them that if they still refused to surrender and continued aggressive action, their villages would be bombed on a certain day and at a certain time. They were instructed to evacuate their village and only return if they were willing to co-operate.

Airmen were held in great esteem by the Arabs, although any who came down and fell into tribal hands were either killed or badly treated in reprisal.

In 1925, a small air contingent was successful in checking an encroachment by the Yemen.

In 1928, a system of air control under Air Force command was set up, whilst in Germany the limitations on the permitted size and number of civilian aircraft were withdrawn. (With hindsight it is clear today that this was a grave error). The German bombers later produced in such numbers by Heinkel and Dornier, together with the Junkers transport aircraft, all began as civilian aircraft.

In the early 1930's, the Disarmament Conference of Geneva was in full swing. One of the proposals put before it was the total abolition of military aircraft, and there were others, such as restrictions on the all-up weight of military aircraft, designed to remove serious offensive power from the bomber.

In Britain, research work into the offensive use of air power had almost ceased, and the RAF was not allowed to order available modern bombers or overtly encourage research and development. The combined effect of the Air Estimates of the Disarmament Conference, the financial crisis of 1931 and the unhelpful attitude of the 'senior' Services was very serious. In addition, stocks of all kinds including bombs, ammunition and spare parts had been allowed to run down to very low levels.

In 1933, Hitler and the Nazi party came to power. The German Sporting Flying Club, the *Deutsche Luftsportverband*, was founded in 1920, and by 1932 had a membership of 60,000. In 1935 the German military air force was officially re-established, its founder membership being drawn from the *Luftsportverband.* A report came from Germany that the German Air Force was equal in size to the RAF, and that conscription in Germany had already been instituted. In the UK, an expansion of the RAF was authorised, but money was short and the aircraft industry hard put to make ends meet.

A new requirement for bombers produced the Whitley, Hampden and Wellington. Harris, now a Group

Captain, was advocating formation flying, as he had in 1926, so that bombers would be better able to defend themselves when returning in daylight or twilight from long distance raids. He was successful and, in 1934-35, 58 and 99 Squadrons were instructed to practise formation flying.

In 1936, Lufthansa made 75 crossings of the South Atlantic, and subsequently over 100, providing valuable experience and practice for the later Dornier flying boats used for reconnaissance work in the early part of WW II.

In Britain, also in 1936, three Commands were formed within the RAF, including Bomber Command. The Wellington bomber made its maiden flight that year, but the requirement for a four-engined heavy bomber[1] was only just being put out to the industry. From this would come first the Stirling, then the Halifax, and the ill-fated Manchester[2].

Harris was to serve on a committee, together with Captain Phillips of the Royal Navy and Colonel Forbes of the Army: they were tasked with compiling a report entitled 'Appreciation of the Situation in the Event of War Against Germany in 1939', and this was submitted to the Chiefs of Staff on 26th October 1936. Prominence was given to the necessity for a strategic bomber force with

[1] - *The decision to develop a four-engined bomber was a fortuitous and an uncommonly far-seeing policy. In Germany the development of the so-called 'Urals Bomber' never found backing and this was to lead to dire consequences, particularly on the Eastern Front, when the Russians moved their main manufacturing capacity beyond the Urals and out of range of the Luftwaffe.*

[2] - ***Avro Manchester*** *- Although this was a twin-engined bomber it is mentioned here because of its obvious lineage resulting in the Lancaster.*

Harris's recommendation that a build-up of aircraft be made to a total of 2,204 by 1939.

In the House of Commons, Mr Winston Churchill stated that Germany had not less than 1,500 first-line aeroplanes in 130 to 140 Squadrons: the RAF had 78 Squadrons.

In September 1937, Himmler said:

> 'In the coming war we shall fight not only on land, on the sea and in the air. There will be a fourth theatre of operations, the 'Inner Front'. That front will decide the continued existence or the irrevocable death of the German nation.'

In 1938, Harris asked for all aircraft on bomber stations to be used for flying practice. A report was sent to Bomber Command by the Air Targets Intelligence Committee, which dealt with power, fuel, chemical, engineering, metallurgical and transportation targets in Germany. It mentioned the possibility of crippling the German war industry by attacking coking plants and power stations in the Ruhr area: the report became Plan W.A.5, and it emphasised the Ruhr's importance as the industrial nerve centre of Germany, producing 75% of national output of coal and iron.

In Spain, the Civil War gave the Germans the chance to learn the art of aerial bombing: thousands of *Luftwaffe* aircrew and hundreds of aircraft had three years of combat experience. The Condor Legion bombed Madrid, Toledo, Bilbao and the Santander Fronts using Heinkel and Henschel aircraft. Professor Haldana made some reasonable calculations, based on the number of bombs dropped in England during WWI and in Barcelona during the Civil War, as to what could be expected in modern warfare with modern aeroplanes. Twenty deaths per ton of bombs dropped were calculated, with the presumed presence of defences and shelters. Thus 500 aircraft, carrying two tons of bombs each, could kill 20,000 people in one single raid.

Effects of Italian and German bombs on Barcelona 1st January 1938. (Imperial War Museum)

In April 1938, in the United Kingdom, Scheme L had received Cabinet approval and would hopefully provide for the production of 12,000 aircraft by 1st April 1940. By virtue of sub-contracting, this plan was well within the resources of the industry. Meanwhile, in Europe, the German army entered Austria and the Sudetenland, and in 1939 Czechoslovakia and Memelland, when 700 German aircraft flew in formation.

On 1st September 1939, Hitler announced from the *Reichstag* in Berlin:

> 'I will not wage war against women or children. I have ordered my Air Force to restrict itself to attacks on military targets.'

That very day his Air Force bombed over 60 towns and villages in Poland, including Warsaw.

The Secretary of State for War, Duff Cooper, asked, 'Are we prepared for unannounced attack?' To his own question he replied: 'We are no more prepared than we are as individuals against murder.'

The Germans were ready to use their bombs as they had used them in Poland, both in co-operation with their armies and in attacks on civilian populations.

CHAPTER FOUR

WORLD WAR TWO

On 1st September 1939, a flight of three Ju87 Stuka aircraft took off to bomb the approaches to a railway bridge over the river Vistula at Dirshau: the invasion of Poland had begun. It was then the turn of Warsaw to be bombed, the beginning of a non-stop campaign lasting 26 days. In that time over 100,000 civilians were killed or injured.

The bomber was then thought of as the weapon to blast a path for the army of the *Blitzkrieg*. In attacks on railway towns, as well as on Warsaw, the civilian population inevitably suffered heavy casualties. In the Polish campaign, Germany used about 40% of her total front line squadrons, amounting to between 1,500 and 2,000 aircraft. The force included 700 bombers, mainly Heinkel III's, Dornier 17's and a small force of Junkers 86's making their first and last contribution as offensive bombers in WWII.

The bombing of Polish airfields was a much greater factor in reducing the Polish Air Force than losses in air combat. Attacks on railways and communications soon followed. The Stuka was used to attack roads and railway junctions, and as a means of disorganising troop movements and retreat, thereby paving the way for pincer movements by the German Army. The bombing was carried out by day as insufficient *Luftwaffe* aircrew had been trained in night operation at that time.

In a series of *Luftwaffe* lectures on the Polish campaign, it was stressed, notably by General Quade, that the terror effect of bombing on civilian moralc was a military factor in air warfare. In a German propaganda film concerning the Polish campaign entitled 'The Baptism of Fire', *Luftwaffe* attacks on military targets were shown with footage of dejected Poles who, in the film, were made to appear very frightened. Germany's reputation as a military power increased immeasurably in Europe following the Polish campaign.

On 3rd September 1939, Mr Chamberlain, the British Prime Minister, made the now historic announcement that England was at war with Germany, having received no satisfactory assurance that German attacks on Poland would cease and that its withdrawal from Polish territory had been carried out. He said later in the House of Commons that it was a sad day for everyone, and even sadder for himself. He went on to say that he hoped to live to see the day when Hitlerism had been destroyed, and a liberated Europe re-established (unfortunately this hope was not to be realised).

At 11.20am on the 3rd, a translation of the reply had been cabled from the American Embassy in Berlin: this was handed to Viscount Halifax at the Foreign Office on 4th September, 1939. The document had been compiled by Herr Joachim von Ribbentrop, Hitler's Foreign Minister, and stated that the German Government and people refused to accept, let alone fulfil, the demands in the Ultimatum made by the British Government, the Treaty of Versailles having torn Germany to pieces. All offers of a peaceful settlement had been refused to every German Government.

The National Socialists had, since 1933, tried again and again to remove, by peaceful negotiation, the most irksome of the clauses of the Treaty[1]. Ribbentrop went on to say that, if the British Government had not intervened, a reasonable solution would have been found between Germany and Poland: Germany had had no intention of annihilating Poland, although the British Government had given the Polish State freedom for all actions against Germany which it might conceivably intend to undertake.

The British Government had assured the Polish Government of its military support in all circumstances, should Germany defend herself against any provocation or attack. The German Government and the German people had assured the English people countless times of their desire for an understanding, indeed close friendship, with them. The statement went on to say that Germany, unlike Great Britain, did not intend to dominate the world, but merely to defend her own liberty, her independence and, above all else, her people's lives. Germany would therefore answer any aggressive action on the part of England with the same weapons and in the same form.

At the outbreak of war with Germany, Scheme L, which had received Cabinet approval in April 1938, and which provided for the production of 12,000 aircraft by April 1st 1940, was in force. Because the new types of aircraft were not ready for production, the Air Council, in October 1938, had decided to place additional orders for existing types so as to make full use of the capacity of the aircraft industry. On 27th September 1939, the War

[1] - *The Treaty of Versailles was commonly known in Germany as the Versailles Diktat. That is, something which is dictated or enforced without the consent of all concerned. Germany had agreed to the armistice which effectively ended WW I, assuming she would be given a place at the negotiating table on similar terms to the Allies. In fact, the terms, as history shows, imposed incredibly punitive conditions and reparations and, perhaps, made WW II inevitable.*

Cabinet approved a monthly rate of 2,300 aircraft, with an additional 250 per month from the Dominions. However, in September 1939, none of the heavy bombers talked about in 1936 had been delivered, and the only aircraft available as bombers were Fairey Battles and Bristol Blenheims, with a few medium bombers such as Whitleys and Wellingtons.

The first German bombs were dropped in October 1939, but no casualties were incurred. Bomber Command policy was that no targets were to be bombed on land: the only targets to be attacked were warships at sea and at anchor, although even those had to be attacked landwards and out to sea. The order was: 'The greatest care is to be taken not to injure the civilian population. The intention is to destroy the German Fleet. There is no alternative target.'

Bombing of this type of target would have to be in daylight, which made the risk of attack by German fighters based in the North Sea area much greater. The respite gained as a result of the expected attacks on the UK in 1939 failing to materialise (as in 1914 during WWI) was a Godsend to Bomber Command. They had a low priority in the pecking order of aircraft supply, particularly in respect of the promised heavy bombers.

In February 1940, a proposed publication to the Press stated that attacks on military objectives by air would put pressure on the manufacturing and industrial resources of Germany. Some people at the time thought that, in these attacks, non-combatants would be killed, and that indiscriminate attacks from the air must be avoided.

The Bombing Restriction Committee was formed in 1940 and recommended that a distinction must be made between the non-combatant pursuing purely civilian occupations, and military objectives with the purpose of transporting troops (such as railway junctions), manufacturing munitions (such as in Essen), or furnishing them with arms (such as at Wilhelmshaven). These civilians, it was argued, were not non-combatants, but were actively and directly sustaining the spear-point of attack. 'Break the shaft as well as parry and blunt the thrust-point of the weapon', was a phrase of the times.

It was proposed that Germany and her local authorities should be warned officially, by leaflet and radio, that her arsenals, marshalling yards, munitions factories, strategic railway centres, bridges and ports were open to attack as legitimate military objectives, and that all women and children should be moved at least ten miles away from such targets.

In March 1940, the first British death from German bombs occurred in the Orkneys. In April 1940 came attacks on Denmark and Norway. Denmark was soon overpowered, but Norway resisted and Britain sent a force to help repel the attacks, although this soon had to withdraw.

The *Luftwaffe* had carried out intensive training for long range bombing, and for both high and low level attacks. On 9th May 1940, bombs were dropped near Canterbury in Kent. On the 10th, Germany invaded Holland, Belgium and Luxembourg. Attacks were made and bombs dropped on the residential district of Brussels, although no declaration of war had been made. The possibility of the bombing of oil refineries and marshalling yards in the Ruhr by Bomber Command was being discussed, but it was decided to wait twenty-four hours.

On 14th May, Rotterdam was bombed: a thousand people were killed, several thousand injured and 78,000 made homeless. The following day the Dutch army laid down its arms.

On 15/16th May 1940, industrial targets in the Ruhr were attacked for the first time. The 'phoney' war was coming to an end, and targets in Yorkshire and in the London District of Addington were bombed.

In June 1940, Harris, now an Air Vice Marshal, was worried about the threat of invasion and the number of barges available on the Continent. 'A thousand,' he said, 'can convey 250,000 German troops, and the large barges on the Rhine could transport armour and guns.'

On 8th July 1940, Churchill sent a letter to Lord Beaverbrook:

> 'When I look to see how we can win this war, I can see there is only one sure path. We have no Continental army which can defeat the German military power. The blockade is broken, and Hitler has Asia and probably Africa to draw from. Should he be repulsed here, or not try invasion, he will recoil eastward and we have nothing to stop them (*sic*). But there is one thing that will bring him back and bring him down, and that is an absolutely devastating, exterminating attack by very heavy bombers from this country upon the Nazi homeland. We must be able to overwhelm them by this means, without which I do not see a way through.'

In his own hand he added:

> 'We cannot accept any lower aim than air mastery. When can it be obtained?'

On the 16th, Hitler issued Directive No 16, 'Preparation for the Invasion of England'. But before this could be put into motion the RAF had to be reduced to a point of little or no resistance.

On 20th August 1940, Winston Churchill delivered

his famous speech to the House of Commons: this became the most famous of the many he made in WWII. Although, over the years, the speech appeared, by the interpretation of the media, to be concerned solely with Fighter Command, it was intended for the RAF as a whole, and one section of it was devoted to Bomber Command:

> 'On no part of the Royal Air Force does the weight of the war fall more heavily than on the daylight bombers, who will play an invaluable part in the case of invasion, and whose unflinching zeal it has been necessary in the meanwhile, on numerous occasions, to restrain. We are able to verify the results of bombing military targets in Germany, not only by reports which reach us through many sources, but also, of course, by photography. I have no hesitation in saying that this process of bombing the military industries and communications of Germany and the air bases and storage depots from which we are attacked, which process will continue upon an ever-increasing scale until the end of the war, and may in another year attain dimensions hitherto undreamed of, affords one at least of the most certain, if not the shortest, of roads to victory. Even if the Nazi Legions stood triumphant on the Black Sea, or indeed upon the Caspian; even if Hitler was at the gates of India, it would profit him nothing if, at the same time, the entire economic and scientific apparatus of German war power lay shattered and pulverised at home.'

Early in July 1940, Churchill had laid down a plan to bomb Berlin if London was attacked: on 24th August 1940 the first bombs fell on the capital. On 25/26th August, 103 Hampden and Whitley bombers set out to bomb Berlin, *'The Big City'*, as the aircrew of Bomber Command came to know it. Many areas other than London had been attacked throughout August 1940, but London seemed to tip the scales.

On 3rd September 1940, Churchill made another speech:

> 'The Navy can lose us the war, but only the Royal Air Force can win it. Therefore our supreme effort must be to gain overwhelming mastery in the air. The fighters are our salvation, but the bombers alone can provide the means of victory. We must therefore develop the power to carry an ever-increasing volume of explosives on Germany, so as to pulverise the entire industry and scientific structure on which the war effort and economic life of the enemy depends, while holding him at arm's length in our island.'

On 4th September 1940, Hitler made a speech ordering attacks on London to commence on 7th September. He said:

> 'If they attack our cities, then we will raze theirs to the ground. We will stop the handiwork of those air pirates, so help us God.'

That same day 300 German bombers attacked London: the *'Battle of London'* had begun, and went on until the end of November. In Germany, Hitler said: 'We shall erase their cities.' The 'Essener Nationalzeitung' followed this up by stating:

'The English people would certainly believe Hitler's words

if they could see the ruins of Warsaw and Rotterdam with their own eyes. London and other English towns will suffer the same fate.'

The 'Stuttgarter Neues Tagblatt' gloated:

'The German people live to see, with the deepest satisfaction, the punishment that is breaking over the guilty in this war. The day of reckoning is here.'

Over 12,000 sorties were flown over the UK, and London received over 13,000 tons of high explosives and nearly one million incendiary bombs. On 19th September 1940, the Air Ministry stated that the object of bombing Berlin was to create maximum demoralisation and dislocation of the community. The main targets were power stations and gas works, and near misses on these targets, which were situated in densely populated areas, would cause casualties to civilians as well as damage to other targets in the vicinity.

On 21st September 1940, 'The Times' Correspondent wrote:

> 'Nine out of ten people of this country prefer not to bomb women or children, but it is very difficult to win a war if the enemy breaks all the rules and we do not. If they use poison gas against our troops, then we must use it against theirs. If we decide never to copy Hitler's evil practices, there is some danger that he may spray London with poison gas, which he certainly will not do if he knows that we should at once retaliate. We must always endeavour to place our bombs on 'Military Objectives', in the widest sense, because it pays. There is, however, great value to be obtained by the broadcast bombing of

> a large city. Sufficient bombs will make its evacuation inevitable, not by killing civilians, but by severing gas and water mains, electric cables and sewers, which are essential to a city's existence. For centuries a beleaguered city has been exposed to artillery bombardment, which is indiscriminate. Long range bombardment is now delivered from the air. London is a beleaguered city; why not Berlin? Our aim must always be to hit 'military objectives' as much as possible, civilians as little as possible, but, now that Germany has become utterly ruthless, it is our duty to win the war as quickly as possible so that the smallest number of our women and children may be murdered by the enemy.'

On the 21st, attacks by Bomber Command had destroyed 12 transport ships, 4 tugs, 51 barges and 9 transports, and damaged 1 tug and 163 barges. The *'Battle of the Barges'* was over and in Germany Hitler postponed the invasion indefinitely.

As well as London, other British cities were under severe attack. On 25th September, Bristol was attacked by 60 bombers with an escort of fighters. They approached from the south and, within minutes, had dropped 90 tons of high explosives mixed with oil bombs. In all, 300 bombs were released over the northern suburbs of the city. In the attack, 41 houses were destroyed and a further 100 left beyond repair, with another 756 damaged. The target was obviously the Filton aircraft works, which was hit by over 160 bombs.

As in all such attacks, the number of casualties was difficult to establish precisely, but it was thought that 72 people were killed and 166 injured: a further 19 were to die later of their injuries. A number of people were also injured, and several ambulances damaged, by delayed action bombs.

In the week ending 2nd October 1940, 2,000 civilians had been killed (1,700 of them in London) and 2,800 wounded. On 5th October, Air Chief Marshal Sir Richard Peirse became Commander-in-Chief of Bomber Command, and Sir Charles Portal became Chief of the Air Staff. Peirse sent a special Order of the Day to all ranks of Bomber Command. In it he said:

> 'The destruction and the achievement of victory falls to the lot of the Royal Air Force. It is Bomber Command in particular, with its power of attack, which today epitomises the determination of the country to carry war to the heart of the enemy. And it shall be so carried.'

On 11th October 1940, information was obtained from a captured *Luftwaffe* pilot, indicating that the German Air Force was to carry out an operation of considerable dimensions against the UK: the code name for this was to be *'Moonlight Sonata'*, which suggested the operation would be at night, and when the moon was full, or nearly so. It indicated that *Luftflotten* (Airfleets) 2 and 3, together with *Kampfgeschwader* 100 (the German Pathfinder Squadron), would be involved, and that the C in C of the German Air Force, Göring, would be in direct control of the operation. The target areas mentioned were:

> **Target Area I**: Possibly Central London, or possibly Norwich or Ipswich.
>
> **Target Area II**: Greater London within the circle Windsor-St Albans, Epping-Gravesend, and Westerham.

Target Area III: Farnborough Aerodrome-Reading -Maidenhead.

Target Area IV: Faversham-Rochester-Sheerness.

Information from other sources suggested the target being either Coventry or Birmingham in the Midlands. On hearing this, the Air Staff issued a counter-plan *'Cold Water'* which included night-fighter forces, intruder activities and the bombing of German airfields and radio beam stations.

On the 15th, the Prime Minister and the Air Ministry made clear that central aims of offensive strategy were the development of Bomber Command as a striking force of overwhelming weight, and an air offensive against objectives in Germany. The bomber force, compared with Germany's, however, was much smaller, and the targets involved much longer flying distances. Also, only seven per cent of the British national war effort was used to build and maintain Bomber Command.

On 14th November 1940, messages were intercepted indicating that *'Moonlight Sonata'* would take place on 14/15th November. The balloon barrage around Coventry was reinforced although, as it happened, no enemy aircraft came below the level of the balloons.

On the night of the 14/15th, 437 German aircraft took off heading towards Coventry: they were in three streams, with ten HE 111's of KG 100 at the head, and were using the *X-Gerat* system, which involved flying along a fine radio beam until a succession of intersecting beams signalled distance to target. The first incendiaries were dropped at 8.15pm, and for the next ten hours the main force released bombs over the blazing city - a total of 503 tons of high explosive, 56 tons of incendiaries and 127 parachute mines. In the attack, 506 were killed, 1,200 injured and 60,000 buildings destroyed, including much of the city centre. Arrangements were made for 10,000 people to be evacuated, but 36 hours later only 300 had left.

The *X-Gerat* beam was later to be successfully 'bent', thus making bombers release their loads in the wrong location, but this was too late for Coventry and its people. The fires in the city were started by incendiary bombs, the type of bomb Hitler had mentioned pre-war, which would set a city alight: Coventry cathedral was destroyed in the attack.

By 6am on the morning of 16th October, the number of those killed by air raids during the previous week was estimated at 1,567, of whom 1,388 had been killed in London. The total number of civilians killed by the end of October was 6,334.

Damage around Coventry Cathedral. (Imperial War Museum).

Damage in the city centre of Coventry. The Pioneer Corps assisted in clearing the debris (Imperial War Museum).

In London, a week after the raid on Coventry, a number of raids were made and several hospitals hit. On 20th December, 136 aircraft attacked London, causing 1,400 fires. In this attack, 60 water mains were burst and supplies ran dry.

The City of London, 29th December 1940. Seen from the dome of St. Paul's Cathedral. (Imperial War Museum).

In 1940, the bomb tonnage dropped by the Germans on the UK was 36,844, as opposed to 14,631 tons dropped on Germany by Bomber Command. Because of poor weather, the attacks were cut from 6,000 in November 1940 to only 1,200 in February 1941.

The City burning, 29th December 1940. (Imperial War Museum).

December 1940. Winston Churchill and Mrs Churchill visit the smoking remains of the Guildhall. (Imperial War Museum).

One of the most famous images of 'The Blitz'. The collapse of No. 23 Queen Victoria Street, 11th May 1941. (Imperial War Museum).

At the Air Ministry, debates were going on as to how the war should be fought. It was suggested that, if it was going to be an open war, then all resources should be primarily bent in that direction. It was felt (not without good reason) that the Bomber Offensive was more of a nuisance than a serious threat.

In November, heavy attacks were made not only on Coventry but also on Birmingham and Southampton, as well as on London, which was still the prime target. In January 1941, 1,550 people were killed and 2,021 injured; in February 793 were killed; and in March a further 4,298 lost their lives. These figures rose dramatically in April and May 1941, when 13,000 were killed. There were further attacks on Coventry in April 1941 and, in five attacks on Plymouth, 750 people were killed and 30,000 made homeless.

Firemen at work in Eastcheap, London, during the night attacks of 1941. (Imperial War Museum).

On 10th May 1941, London was attacked by 320 bombers, the attack lasting five hours. The major problem was water pressure, 55 water mains having been burst, which required the Fire Service to set into every known alternative source and use every available pump. In all, more than 2,000 fires were started, of which 10 were declared major and 43 serious: 14 hospitals were hit, including the Children's Hospital in Westminster. In

Bermondsey the Mayor was killed when the Town Hall was hit.

The attack claimed 1,400 killed and 1,800 injured: 1,724 HE bombs were dropped, of which 162 did not explode. In tackling the fires, over 2,000 fire engines were used, 16 firemen were killed and 250 were injured. As well as hospitals, churches and schools, the House of Commons was hit and set on fire. The only building not on fire, according to eye-witnesses, was St Paul's Cathedral. The next day never became fully daylight because of the fires and smoke.

All Hallows Church, Barking, three years after its destruction on 29th December 1940. Like many blitzed sites, it was converted into a garden of rest. (Imperial War Museum).

This turned out to be the last serious raid on London for three years. The Blitz had ended, but not before 44,000 people had been killed and 103,000 injured between August 1940 and May 1941. German Air Force losses had reached serious proportions, as it had trained primarily for night bombing. Somehow, the opening defensive phase of the war had been weathered.

On 22nd June 1941, Hitler invaded Russia, upon which event Churchill declared:

> 'Any man or state who fights against Russia will have our aid. We shall bomb Germany by day and night in ever increasing measure, casting on them, month by month, a heavier discharge of bombs and making the German people taste and gulp each month a sharper dose of misery than they have showered upon mankind. We shall give whatever help we can to Russia and to the Russian people. This is no class war. This is a war in which the whole British Empire and Commonwealth of Nations is engaged without distinction of race, creed, or party.'

However, after an investigation in June/July 1941, known as the Butt Report, it was revealed that only one-fifth of Bomber Command aircraft despatched were dropping their bombs within five miles of the target. The Ruhr area became known to bomber crews, with grim irony, as 'Happy Valley' (because of its heavy flak defences and great concentrations of searchlights), and there it appeared that only 7% of the aircraft bombed within five miles of the target.

This seemed to diminish Churchill's opinion that bombing would be a decisive factor in the war. He was also influenced by the effects the German attacks had already had on London and the rest of the country, and would have in future. Civilian morale was a vital weapon in the German arsenal and, therefore, an equally important factor for the Allies.

CHAPTER FIVE

BOMBER COMMAND AND ITS CREWS

When the war began, in September 1939, the strength of Bomber Command was 30 Squadrons, with 16 aircraft in each Squadron. Over 40% were light bombers, the Fairey Battle and the Blenheim. The remaining 60% were medium bombers, the Wellington, Hampden and Whitley.

The Squadrons were divided into five operational groups:

No 1 Group (Fairey Battles)
No 2 Group (Blenheims)
No 3 Group (Wellingtons)
Nos 4 and 5 Groups (Hampdens)

Each Squadron had an Officer Commanding who was himself a pilot and, although OC's were only required to fly four operations per month, many flew far more.

The central point of any Bomber Station was the Control Tower, or Watch Tower, as it was also known, a grey utility building in the middle of the airfield, surrounded by the runways. It was manned around the clock by three radio transmitter operators, three officers and three ground crew. The day shift was from 8am to 5pm and the night shift from 5pm to 8am. Each Squadron would have its own call-sign which its aircraft would use on take-off and on returning to land. The Operations Room was manned 24 hours a day, 52 weeks of the year, requiring a minimum of three WAAF watch-keepers rotating on a 24 hour shift.

A briefing took place before each operation in which

the target, the plan of attack, outward and return routes and intelligence about defences at the target and en route were all fully covered.

On return (for those who did return) there was a debriefing. The crews were asked about the defences, the type of flak encountered and any contact with fighters: all this information would be collated and used when the same target was attacked at a later date.

The ground crews on a Bomber Station were vital, not only for keeping the aircraft serviced, but in loading the bombs and the guns before each operation. The task was being carried out all over Yorkshire, Lincolnshire, Cambridgeshire and East Anglia, with up to 20 aircraft and 140 men from each station to get into the air for up to five days every working week for several months. Over a period of, say, five months this would amount to 100 days of continuous operations, involving some 2,000 sorties: the crews also had to be fed and transported to their aircraft.

A large Bomber Station would have a personnel establishment of up to 2,000 men and women. These stations were like villages or small towns, with the Squadron resembling a hotel, and the crews the guests. Sadly, many of the guests who came did not stay very long, and made the one-way trip which ended in the ultimate sacrifice.

It was Royal Air Force policy that staff officers should not become detached from the fighting men as they had in WWI. Often, Squadron Commanders worked as staff officers for six months or so, then returned as Station Commanders. The respect of the men being sent out night after night came from knowing that the great majority of the officers responsible had been there before them, and knew at first hand the dangers and problems they would face. 'Never ask a man to do something you have not done yourself,' could have been the motto of Bomber Command in World War II.

All RAF aircrew were volunteers: men could be conscripted into the Air Force, but not made to fly. As so many men were needed for Bomber Command, it was inevitable that many who did volunteer for aircrew ended up there. Only thirteen out of every hundred of these volunteers who served with Bomber Command survived the war.

The training, which could take anything up to 18 months, was carried out in the USA, Canada, South Africa and, of course, Britain. The ages of the crews averaged 21, but there were some men in their 30's, who were regarded as quite elderly - almost father-figures - by their crewmates. At the other end of the scale were men who had falsified their ages and were flying at sixteen: one man was, in fact, a prisoner-of-war in Germany at that age. One eighteen-year-old was killed flying on the famous Dambuster raid of May 1943: it was his 30th operation.

The method of getting a crew together was remarkable, but somehow it worked, and worked well. They simply gathered together in a hangar or crew room and chose each other: 'I need a gunner. Will you fly with me?' was the general line of conversation. With this system, not only did seven men make up a crew but, in the majority of cases, they became as efficient as if they had been hand-picked.

A tour of operations was, at the beginning, 25 to 30 missions. But, in many cases, if a crew completed five it was lucky. Even if crew members survived being shot down, there was the prospect of being held prisoner for a number of years. Each trip they faced not only flak and fighters, but also bad weather and engine malfunction.

The men came from all over the world - Canada, Australia, New Zealand, South Africa, the West Indies and the USA: a number of Americans served in the RCAF and the RAF before the USA came into the war officially. They came from all walks of life, and vastly different educational backgrounds, ranging from the basic to public school or university. This all mattered little, the seemingly most unlikely mix of men often integrating into successful crews: the better the team, the better the chances of survival.

There was another fear, that of being graded LMF (Lack of Moral Fibre). Some, having flown a number of operations, simply could not go on, and felt that, if they did, they would endanger the rest of the crew. The main impact on a man unfortunate enough to be rated LMF was the sense of loss of confidence of his Commanding Officer. Many medical officers were sympathetic, and men were grounded for other medical reasons but, for some, the consequences of refusing to fly again were severe. LMF personnel were taken off the Station and posted to an Aircrew Disposal Unit which, at first, was based at Uxbridge. Then, when this proved unsatisfactory, they were sent to Eastchurch, then to Ulsworth and finally to Keresley Grange, Coventry. The term 'Lack of Moral Fibre' was thought by some in Bomber Command to be too severe and inappropriate. They considered it implied complete cowardice when, in fact, 'moral fibre' meant a particular kind of courage required for the control of fear of flying duties: a man might have been prepared to exercise the self control required to face up to the hazards of the sea or on the land, but not in the air.

Before taking off on an operation, the pilot would have to make numerous pre-flight checks. Some were external, for instance ensuring the covers were removed from the pitot head and static vents, that the tyres were properly inflated and that there was no sign of 'creep', and that there were no leaks of hydraulic fluids, oil or fuel:

These checks were laconically described as, 'counting the wings and kicking the tyres'.

After the pre-start up checks had been completed with the flight engineer, the engines would be started, first the port inner to provide hydraulic pressure to raise the flaps and close the bomb doors, followed by the others, one at a time. Then would come the after-start up check on temperatures and pressures, and the all important 'mag drop' as each individual engine's two magnetos were tested. The pre-take off checks would follow: auto controls, compass, fuel, flaps and so on until the full check list had been run.

Elsewhere in the aircraft the other members of the crew had their own tasks to attend to, some on take off, others en route, and yet more on the approach to and over the target; a team working harmoniously to keep a complex machine airborne, on course and, as far as possible, unmolested.

In 1940, a young airman serving in Bomber Command wrote a letter, to be sent to his mother if he failed to return. This was published in 'The Times' on 18th June 1940:

'Today we are faced with the greatest organised challenge to Christianity and civilisation the world has ever seen, and I count myself lucky and honoured to be of the right age and fully trained to throw my full weight into the scale... I have no fear of death.

The universe is so vast and so ageless that the life of one man can only be justified by the measure of his sacrifice.'

Pilot Officer Rosewane called his quest in Bomber Command a 'Fight With Evil And That His Earthly Mission Was Fulfilled.'

> 'Dear Mother,
> Though I feel no premonition at all, events are moving rapidly, and I have instructed that this letter be forwarded to you should I fail to return from one of the raids we shall shortly be called upon to undertake. You must hope on for a month, but at the end of that time you must accept the fact that I have handed my task over to the extremely capable hands of my comrades of the Royal Air Force, as so many splendid fellows have already done. I have always admired your amazing courage in the face of continual setbacks; in the way you have given me as good an education and background as anyone in the country; and always kept up appearances without ever losing faith in the future. My death would not mean that your struggle has been in vain. Far from it. It means your sacrifice is as great as mine. Those who serve England must expect nothing from her; we debase ourselves if we regard our country as merely a place in which to eat and sleep.'

These are examples of the type of men who served in Bomber Command.

Today, the men who survived those events of fifty years ago are now in their seventies, and many are grandfathers. For them to explain now what they were doing then is not easy in such a different world and situation. Their actions helped to prevent Britain and the rest of the world from being taken over by the Nazis, a fate which would have been worse than death.

These young men, some with just three stripes on their arm (Sergeant eventually becoming the minimum rank for aircrew) grew up quickly, matured overnight and lived a life in which one night was spent over the heart of enemy territory, and the next at the local pub. They were like springs, wound fully for an operation and unwinding when they returned, time after time. The soldier at the battle Front gets used to a sustained pitch of combat and the knowledge that he will remain at the Front for some time. The bomber crewman knew he was going into battle one day and coming out the next, day after day and night after night.

Crews were coming and going constantly to replace those who went missing: frequently there were empty beds in the billets, with Service Police clearing out the kit of the men who did not return. Nobody really got to know those with whom they served very well: Smith was Smudge, White was Chalky and so on. Little else was known about a man other than whether he was a good pilot, engineer, navigator or air gunner. Now, fifty years on, many ex-bomber men are trying to trace former members of their crews.

They gave all they had, and were willing to give the most precious possession of all - their lives - in the cause of keeping the world free from a dictatorship which they abhorred.

CHAPTER SIX

THE HARRIS ERA

On 8th January 1942, Air Marshal Sir Richard Peirse, C in C Bomber Command, was relieved of his position. In November 1941, on an operation to Berlin, 37 aircraft failed to return and Peirse was asked for an explanation by Churchill, via Portal. The result was not acceptable, and it seemed that, from then on, a replacement was being sought.

On 22nd February 1942, Sir Arthur Harris became C in C Bomber Command. He soon found that the Command had, effectively, no more aircraft than when the war had started in September 1939.

The policy of the Government had been, after the fall of France, to carry out a strategic bombing campaign against Germany, with the aim of the progressive destruction of German war industries and morale, in order to set the scene for future re-entry to Europe. With this policy, it was expected that the build-up of Bomber Command aircraft would be the highest priority but, as fast as they becamc available, they were being sent to other Commands, such as Coastal, and to other theatres of war, such as the Middle East. Hundreds of aircraft were being flown out to Egypt by Bomber Command crews, and there they stayed, unused.

The Command had about 370 aircraft and an average lift of about 700 tons of bombs, but its expansion was outweighed by losses to other Commands. With 117 ships totalling 750,000 tons having been sunk in the Atlantic, disasters in the Far East and setbacks in the Middle East, there was an outcry in Britain to send aircraft abroad, and everywhere the call was for bombers.

Sir Arthur Harris. From a painting found in the Public Records Office, now at RAF Museum Hendon.

It was up to Harris and his SASO, Air Vice Marshal Saundby, to decide whether the bombers should be transferred to other Commands and theatres from which they would not return. On 20th February 1942, there were twenty-six medium bomber squadrons, consisting of Hampdens, Wellingtons and Whitleys, but only seven heavy squadrons: three had Manchesters, two Stirlings, two Halifaxes, but, as yet, there were no Lancasters. Added to these were two Special Duty squadrons of Wellingtons, Halifaxes and Lysanders, making thirty-five squadrons in all.

The introduction of 'Gee' was the first major move away from navigators having to rely on the sextant as the sole means of navigation. This new method was designed to improve the standard of navigation at night, to permit blind bombing and to identify targets at night under operational conditions. The decision to use Gee had come in August 1941, but it was suspended on the grounds that the Germans might use jamming counter-measures. Until Bomber Command was fully equipped and in a position to make full use of Gee, it was left unused. In 1942, ten squadrons had been equipped and trained in the use of Gee and on the 8/9th March 1942, it was used operationally for the first time, against Essen. Although it improved accuracy generally, it was not very effective over the Ruhr, and visual identification was still necessary for accurate bombing. The chief target in the Ruhr was Essen, but industrial haze made visual identification difficult or even impossible.

In March 1942, Lord Trenchard wrote to the Prime Minister, Winston Churchill, concerning morale in Britain, and in the RAF in particular. He stated that, in his opinion, 99% of bombs were being wasted, together with a similar proportion of the crews, their training, and all the machinery, labour and material that went into their production. This went even deeper, in that 99% of all the ships which had transported the raw materials, and the finance to produce those materials, was being wasted in equal measure. If, however, the same bombs were accurately dropped in Germany, then the high percentage which missed the military targets would all help to kill, damage, frighten or generally disrupt life in Germany so that the entire bomber organisation would be doing useful work, and not merely one per cent. Trenchard advocated persistent bombing of military targets in every town in Germany without respite. He went on to say that this should be carried out every single night, and on most days, when weather conditions were favourable. A great force should, he argued, be sent to destroy military objectives of primary importance.

The object of the night and day bombing of military targets in Germany was to make the civilian population realise what going to war meant, and to make them aware that, if there was a military objective in every town, it was liable to be attacked. Trenchard regarded this as the only effective way in which the enemy could be hit and victory achieved for the assembled forces.

On 28/29th March 1942, the port of Lübeck, in the Baltic, was attacked by 234 aircraft of which 43 were heavy bombers: 144 tons of incendiaries and 160 tons of high explosive were dropped in two waves, with an interval of half an hour. The justification for targeting Lübeck was that it was being used as a supply base for the German occupation forces in Norway, and as a forward supply base for the Russian front. The port itself, together with the surrounding warehouses, was full of supplies waiting for the Spring, when the ice could be cleared from the channel and the accumulated material ferried across the Baltic. At the time of the attack the channel was still not clear of ice.

During the attack, the Dragerwerk factory, which made oxygen equipment for U-Boats and aircraft, was destroyed. Much of the damage to the port was caused by fire. It was the heaviest raid on a German town since the war had begun: over 2,000 houses were destroyed and a dozen factories destroyed or damaged. Up to 320 people were killed in the attack, the heaviest toll of casualties thus far in the war in Germany. RAF losses were 12 aircraft missing. The port was completely out of action for some three weeks, and its effectiveness impaired for some time.

Goebbels recorded in his diary that the damage was really enormous and that that sort of raid could, if continued, have an effect on the population of towns and cities.

Harris is known to have said: 'Some people say that bombing could never win a war: well, we shall see.'

The attack on Lübeck was followed between 23rd and 27th April by four attacks on the Baltic port of Rostock, mounted again to prevent the port being used for supplies intended for the Russian front and to put out of action the important ring of Heinkel aircraft factories in and around Rostock itself. In 1939, the influx of skilled workers for the factories had brought the population of Rostock up to 115,000. Since then the figure had risen.

For the bomber crews, it was a 550 mile trip to Rostock, and the target was expected to be as well defended as anywhere else in Germany. In the attack, the whole port and town became a beacon of fire which guided other bombers to the small target, and to the main assembly shed of the principal Heinkel factory. Large fires were observed throughout the whole town, at the Heinkel works and in the Neptune shipyards and warehouses along the waterfront. In the attack 240 people were killed, although many more would have died if they had not fled the city after the previous raids. Goebbels wrote in his diary: 'Community life in Rostock is nearly at an end.'

It was after these raids that the word *'Terrorangriff'*, meaning 'Terror Raid', was first used in German reports; the airmen of Bomber Command soon became known as

'Terrorflieger' or 'Terror Flyers.'

On 4th May, Harris replied to a letter from Air Marshal Peck at the Air Ministry on the subject of Lübeck. It appeared that Peck had heard that the aircrew of Bomber Command were unhappy about the attack on Lubeck. Harris replied that his information was that the aircrew were glad to give the Boche a dose of his own medicine, and that they proposed to give more of it. He related a story from the early campaigns in the Middle East, of the armoured-car gunner who had seemed depressed by the fearful slaughter he had witnessed the previous day, when two armoured-cars had written off Ibn Saud's invading army. He had reassured this gunner that he had only been doing his duty, whereupon the gunner replied: 'I wasn't worried about that: I was wondering what I'd have done if I'd run out of ammunition at half time.'

In the four attacks on Rostock only eight aircraft failed to return to base.

German war industry generally operated by means of a main factory with several subsidiary sheds and garage workshops in the town: many of the latter would have been destroyed in the attack, whilst the main Heinkel factory was hit by at least three bombs, which went through the main assembly shed. One hole was 70 feet across and the other 250 feet.

A final daylight photographic reconnaissance sortie showed more than seventy destroyed and damaged Heinkel bomber fuselages which the Germans had dragged out of the wrecked assembly sheds. The experimental assembly sheds and other aircraft factories suffered direct hits, and the main offices, including the drawing office, were damaged by fire. The Marienehe aerodrome, just outside the factory, had white crosses displayed prohibiting landing because of the extensive damage caused during the raid.

In order to give a practical demonstration of what

could be done if Bomber Command were expanded to a reasonable size, a large raid was required. Harris had said to Saundby:

> 'We shall never get anywhere at this rate. If only we could send a thousand bombers over Germany every good night, we should soon get on with the job.'

He repeated this at a later date with three objectives in mind.

1. To prove that the damage done by 1,000 aircraft would be far greater, and that the fire fighters and civil defence organisations in Germany would be unable to cope.

2. To saturate enemy defences, thereby reducing losses to the attacking aircraft.

3. To show that a force of this size could be handled and controlled in the air.

On 5th May 1942, Gee trials were carried out in the Leeds/Doncaster area, with aircraft of five squadrons taking part. On 18th May, Harris discussed his plan with Portal. However, to amass 1,000 aircraft would require taking some from OTU's and some from conversion flights: Coastal Command would also need to release aircraft to make up the numbers. On the 19th he was given the go-ahead, having demonstrated that 700 aircraft would come from within Bomber Command and the remainder from the other sources.

On the 20th, he wrote to all units in Bomber Command, Coastal Command, Flying Training Command

and Army Co-operation Command, outlining his plan and enlisting their support. He received an immediate and enthusiastic response. The OTU's promised to provide 300 aircraft manned by instructors and certain selected pupils, so within Bomber Command he had the 700 he had anticipated. However, he still needed a further 300, and therefore Saundby hoped that the bomber aircraft given to Coastal Command would be made available.

The operation would need good weather and a full moon, with so many aircraft taking part. Two dates that seemed most suitable were 27/28th or 30/31st May, the target being either Hamburg or Cologne depending on the weather.

Provision of 250 aircraft had been promised on behalf of Coastal Command by the C in C, but was overruled by the Royal Navy which, at the time, controlled Coastal. Despite this, Harris was able to assemble a total of 1,047 aircraft.

On the 24th Harris sent a message to be read out at the crew briefings:

> 'The force of which you form a part tonight is at least twice the size, and has more than four times the carrying capacity of the largest air force ever before concentrated on one objective. You have an opportunity, therefore, to strike a blow at the enemy which will resound, not only throughout Germany, but throughout the world. Next to London, New York and Liverpool, Hamburg is the most important commercial and industrial port in the world. It is also, however, the main centre of Germany's submarine building and manning activities, the very focus of German nautical tradition and a vast hive of general war industry. In your hands lies the means of

> destroying a major part of the resources by which the enemy's war effort are maintained. It depends, however, upon each individual crew whether full concentration is achieved. Press home your attack to your precise objective with the utmost determination and resolution, in the foreknowledge that, if you individually succeed, the most shattering and devastating blow will have been delivered against the very vitals of the enemy.
> Let him have it right on the chin.'

Because of the weather in the area of Hamburg on the 27/28th, the target became Cologne. It was a city of immense importance to the German railway system. The factories producing heavy engines and chemicals were also very important to the enemy's war effort.

The city was heavily defended, with 120 searchlights and about 500 anti-aircraft guns. To get the bombers there to deliver their 1,500 tons of bombs would take 2,000,000 gallons of petrol and 70,000 gallons of oil, with the guns on the aircraft being loaded with 10,000,000 rounds of ammunition for protection. The crews would consume, en route, 8,000 pints of coffee and 6,000lbs of food.

Take-off was set for 22.30hrs and 1,047 aircraft were able to get off the ground - a very high percentage indeed. One of those flying, with a crew of 218 Squadron, was Air Vice Marshal Baldwin, AOC 3 Group. He had last bombed Cologne in August 1918, on which occasion a total of 30 bombs had been dropped.

Of the 1,047 aircraft which had taken off, 898 (86%) claimed to have reached the target and bombed it. The rescue services on the ground were swamped by 1,455 tons of bombs, comprising 540 tons of HE and 915 tons of incendiaries; 12,000 fires were started and 45,000 people were left homeless; over 600 acres of the city were devastated; over 250 factories were either destroyed or damaged, together with a number of oil storage depots. In the 36 factories not destroyed or damaged, production ceased completely.

Cologne Cathedral in 1945. The colossal damage to the city centre is still very apparent. (Private collection).

A German soldier was heard to say: 'Life is coming off the rails.' In Cologne, refugees shouted at the Minister of the Interior: 'This is the bill for London that we are paying! This is the revenge for Coventry!'

A grim joke at the time concerned a man who was condemned to death: when asked to select the means of his execution, he suggested that becoming a flak gunner might be the quickest.

The anger of the people was fuelled by the fact that neither Hitler, Göring or Goebbels attended the funerals of those killed in the attack.

The casualties were relatively light, considering the zeal of the raid, 500 people being killed. However, the entire rescue service had to be reorganised because so many personnel had been killed or injured, and it had been impossible to deal with the fires.

Bomber Command lost 40 aircraft (3.8%) - comparatively few considering the number taking part. Of those missing 16 were known to have been shot down by flak and 4 by fighters; 2 were lost in collisions and the fate of the remainder was unknown. In previous attacks on Cologne, between August 1941 and April 1942, average losses were 3.5%.

Nine days after the raid, Cologne was still cut off from communication by telephone with the rest of Germany, and no mail was allowed to go out for two weeks: even then it was heavily censored. It took thousands of soldiers, prisoners of war and conscript labour ten days to clear the streets of rubble.

After the raid Harris sent a message to the German people by means of dropping leaflets:

> 'We in Britain know quite well enough about air raids. For ten months your Luftwaffe has bombed us. First you bombed us by day. When we made this impossible, they came by night. Then they had a big fleet of bombers. Your airmen fought well. They bombed London for 92 nights running. They made heavy raids on Coventry, Plymouth, Liverpool and other British cities. They did a lot of damage. Forty-three thousand British men, women and children lost their lives. Many of our most cherished historical buildings were destroyed. You thought, and

Göring promised you, that you would be safe from bombs. And indeed, during all that time, we could only send over a small number of aircraft in return. But now it is just the other way. Now you send only a few aircraft against us, and we are bombing Germany heavily. Why are we doing so? It is not revenge - though we do not forgive Warsaw, Belgrade, Rotterdam, London, Plymouth and Coventry. We are bombing Germany, city by city, and ever more terribly, in order to make it impossible for you to go on with the war. That is our object. We shall pursue it remorselessly, city by city: Lübeck, Rostock, Cologne, Emden, Bremen, Wilhelmshaven, Duisberg, Hamburg - and the list will grow longer and longer. Let the Nazis drag you down to disaster with them if you will. That is for you to decide. In fine weather we bomb you by night. Already one thousand bombers go to one town, like Cologne, and destroy a third of it in an hour's bombing. We know, we have the photographs. In cloudy weather we bomb your factories and shipyards by day. We have done that as far away as Danzig. We are coming by day and by night. No part of the Reich is safe. In Cologne, on the Ruhr, or at Rostock, Lübeck or Emden, you may feel that already our bombing amounts to something. But we do not think so. In comparison with what it will be like as soon as our own production of bombers comes to a flood, and as American production doubles and then redoubles, all that has happened to you so far will seem very little. I will speak frankly to you about whether we bomb single military targets or whole cities. Obviously we prefer to hit factories, shipyards and railways. It damages Hitler's war machine most. But those people who work in these plants live close to them. Therefore we hit your houses and you. We regret the necessity for this. The workers of Humboldt-Deutz, the Diesel - engine plant in Cologne, for instance, some of whom were killed on the 30th May last, must inevitably take the risk of war. Just as our merchant seamen who man ships which the U-Boats (equipped with Humboldt-Deutz engines) would have tried to torpedo. Were not the aircraft workers, their wives and children at Coventry just as much 'civilians' as the aircraft workers at Rostock and their families? But Hitler wanted it that way. It is true that your defences inflict losses on our bombers. Your leaders try to comfort you by telling you that our losses are so heavy that we shall not be able to go on bombing you very much longer. Whoever believes that will be bitterly disappointed. I, who command the British bombers, will tell you what our losses are. Less than 5% of the bombers which we send over Germany are lost. Such a percentage of loss does very little even to check the constant increase ensured by the ever-increasing output of our own and the American factories. America has only just entered the fight in Europe. The first squadrons, forerunners of a whole air fleet, have arrived in England from the USA. Do you realise what it will mean to you when they bomb Germany also?

In one American factory alone, the new Ford plant at Willow Run, Detroit, they are already turning out one four-engine bomber, able to carry four tons of bombs to any part of the

Reich, every two hours. There are scores of other such factories in the USA. You cannot bomb those factories. Your submarines cannot even try to prevent those American bombers from getting here. For they fly across the Atlantic. Soon we shall be coming every night and every day, rain, blow or snow, we and the Americans. I have just spent 8 months in America, so I know exactly what is coming. We are going to scourge the Third Reich from end to end, if you make it necessary for us to do so. You cannot stop it, and you know it. You have no chance. You could not defeat us in 1940 when we were almost unarmed and stood alone. Your leaders were crazy to attack Russia as well as America. But then your leaders are crazy: the whole world thinks so, excepting Italy. How can you hope to win, now that we are getting ever stronger, having both Russia and America as allies, whilst you are getting more and more exhausted? One final thing. It is up to you to end the war and the bombing. You can overthrow the Nazis and make peace. It is not true that we plan a peace of revenge. That is a German propaganda lie. But we shall certainly make it impossible for any German Government to start a total war again. And that is as necessary in your own interests as in ours.
Signed - Harris.'

During the course of the summer of 1942, two more thousand-bomber raids were carried out: to Essen on 1st/2nd June, and to Bremen on 25/26th June. However, the strain on the training organisation was too great to allow such raids to be carried out on a regular basis.

Sir Arthur Harris and family. Released for publication 15th June 1943.

Another family photograph, apparently taken some time later. (Both photographs given to the author by Harris).

In August 1942 came a big break-through in the air war. The Pathfinder Force was formed, under an Australian Group Captain (later Air Vice Marshal), Don Bennett. The force was formed from experienced crews within Bomber Command, their task being to locate, mark and keep marked the target for the Main Force bombers following the Pathfinders.

The system of 'illumination' and 'fire raising' was not a new one: the Germans had used it against the UK in 1940/41.

The crews who flew in the Pathfinder Force had to volunteer for 45 operations: this total included previous pre-Pathfinder Operations with a Main Force Squadron.

The scene was now set for an all-out Bomber Offensive on Germany.

CHAPTER SEVEN

BOMBER OFFENSIVE

The effect Bomber Command was having on the war took a major step forward when, following the introduction of Gee, came OBOE, a device designed to assist navigation and bombing accuracy. It worked with the aid of two ground stations: one kept the aircraft flying along a pre-determined track, and the second (the master station) made periodic measurements of distance from which the ground speed of the aircraft was calculated and the correct moment of bomb release determined and signalled. However, the disadvantage of OBOE was its limited range, this being only 300 miles - ideal for targets in the Ruhr but no further. It was first used successfully in December 1942.

The medium bomber squadrons had been replaced by heavy bombers, consisting of Halifax and Lancaster aircraft. With this transformation, bomb carrying capacity rose sharply and, by the summer of 1943, it became possible to deliver 2,000 tons of bombs in full-scale raids on Germany. To combat this increase came much heavier German fighter defences: 85% of the enemy's night fighter force and 50% of his day fighters were now based in Western France. Added to this was the vast increase in strength of the enemy's air defences, every effort having been made to improve equipment. The latest radio location systems for control of night fighters, radar directed flak guns and searchlights had been provided in vast quantities. This increase and development in defences had caused attacks on vital objectives in Germany to become more difficult week by week. Much thought was being given to outwitting the enemy by means of improved tactics, and by the introduction of counter-measures to jam and interfere with the radio control systems essential to his night air defences.

From the beginning of 1943, when the Strategic Air Offensive began, the control of the Allied Strategic Air Force in Europe rested with the Combined Chiefs of Staff: the Chief of the Air Staff, Sir Charles Portal, acted as sole agent in the direction and co-ordination of the effect of the heavy bombers.

Sandhurst Road School, Catford, London, 20th January 1943. Rescue workers try to reach children buried in the rubble following a daylight attack. Forty-four people were killed, including thirty-eight children. (Imperial War Museum)

On 21st January 1943, the Combined Chiefs of Staff Directive made the bombing and disorganisation of German war industry a priority, followed by U-Boat building yards, aircraft industries and transport and oil targets.

At the Casablanca Conference in January 1943, it was decided that strategic bombing should be used to prepare for a future land invasion, and that a combined bomber offensive with the Americans, under the code name Point-Blank, be aimed at depriving the enemy of resources in his factories: it was thought that this would ultimately bring victory in Europe.

Winston Churchill returns from Casablanca. On his right is Air Chief Marshal Sir Charles Portal, Chief of the Air Staff. (Imperial War Museum).

The German war industry relied heavily on its civilian workers in the factories: they did not wear a uniform, but were as much soldiers and fighting men and women as those in uniform at the Front. In any war, innocent people will always be killed together with those directly involved: that is a fact which cannot be altered or eradicated, no matter what plans or organisational changes are implemented to prevent it.

On 5th March 1943, the bomber offensive really began. The first major attack was on Essen in the Ruhr and, in particular, the Krupps armaments factory. Later in history this campaign became known as the 'Battle of the Ruhr'.

The factory covered an area of 800 acres, the combined size of Kensington Gardens, Hyde, Green and St James's Parks in London, or Central Park in New York. It employed 150,000 workers of whom 80,000 were in the main plant. The area was defended by no less than 1,000 heavy guns, 2,000 light guns and 500 searchlights. In fact, the total defences of this factory were greater than those deployed in the whole of Tunisia in North Africa, whilst the nightfighter station in the area possessed three times as many aircraft. In the first attack, thirteen of the main buildings were virtually destroyed and several smaller factories partially gutted. The municipal tram depot, which was the town's main source of transport, was also destroyed. In the residential area, 450 acres were devastated.

Four weeks later factory production showed only 50% of its normal output. Locomotive production stopped altogether and did not restart. Absenteeism in the factories increased to 50% after the 5th. Manufacturing of fuses, large shells, guns, gun tubes and liners stopped for some four months, or fell to half production after the 5th.

In 1943 came H2S which greatly advanced the range of OBOE. The H2S sets were known as 'Y' sets, and gave a picture on a screen derived from a beam which was transmitted towards the ground. The echoes or reflections returned to the aircraft on a Plan Position Indicator (PPI). The quality of the picture was determined primarily by the shape and strength of the tracking beam, and, secondly, by

the nature of the reflecting surface.
The sets were to be used mainly in raids on Berlin, the narrower beam picking out the lakes in and around the city which were used as reference points to drop markers.

The Navy was anxious to obtain most of the sets for the 'Battle of the Atlantic', but Don Bennett (OC the Pathfinders) made sure that he got the first hundred, leaving the remainder for Coastal Command and the Navy.

On 27th May 1943, Hamburg was listed as a major target in Bomber Command Operation Order No 173. It was the second largest city in Germany, and its total destruction would achieve immeasurable results in reducing the industrial capacity of the enemy's war machine. This, together with the effect on German morale, would play a very important part in shortening and winning the war. The 'Battle of Hamburg', as it became known, could not be won in a single night, and it was anticipated that at least 10,000 tons of bombs would have to be dropped to complete the process of elimination.

On 17th July 1943, a Bomber Command Memo stated that 'Window'[1] was to be used for the first time as a counter-measure against the defence system.

Also on the 17th, the then Archbishop of Canterbury received a letter from Sir Archibald Sinclair, Secretary of State for War. On the 9th, the Archbishop had written to the Minister questioning the bombing policy adopted in the war so far. The reply stated that there had been no change in the policy, and that in no part did it include the wanton destruction of cities regardless of military objectives, as the German Air Force had attempted in the 'Baedeker' raids. The intention was, rather, to deprive the enemy of weapons,

[1] - ***'Window'*** *- Strips of aluminum foil cut to half the wave-length of the enemy radar. Dropped in bundles these strips gave a confusing picture to the enemy's radar operators.*

munitions, transportation resources and all the complex apparatus without which fighting forces were powerless.

Sinclair's reply continued:

> 'These military objectives are dotted about in the heart of the industrial cities. We cannot attack factories without damaging surrounding buildings. These cities are not only military arsenals, but heavily defended fortresses. In Germany there are more than 500 night fighters, along with 3,000 Anti-Aircraft guns and 1,000 searchlights. What we cannot do is refrain from attacking an important military objective because it is situated near old and beautiful buildings.'

On 10th April 1943, Goebbels said at the height of the 'Battle of the Ruhr':

> 'No one can tell how long Krupps can go on. There will be no purpose in doing so for the moment, as Essen is no longer an industrial centre. The English will pounce upon the next city: Bochum, Dortmund or Dusseldorf.'

On 24th July 1943, Portal stated in a Memorandum that an attack on Hamburg was being planned, its ship building yards, engineering factories and liquid fuel depots being the main objectives. On the evening of 24/25th July, came an all-out attack on the city. A total of 791 aircraft was despatched, each carrying bundles of 'Window' type 'A'. Each bundle weighed 2lbs and consisted of 2,000 'tinfoil' strips, each strip being 30cm long by 1.5cm wide and 0.1cm thick: one bundle was despatched from each aircraft every minute, which meant that roughly two and a half million strips, or 20 tons, were discharged. Each bundle reflected an echo for fifteen minutes, the time it took to reach the ground: the total number of echoes on the German radar screens during the raid would have corresponded to about 12,000 aircraft.

Preparations for a raid on Hamburg. Before any raid nobody worked harder than the armourers. (Imperial War Museum).

In the four major attacks on Hamburg in July 1943, all four main ship-building yards, including the U-Boat yards, were destroyed or severely damaged. In his diary for July Goebbels wrote: 'If the English continue these raids on this scale they will make it exceedingly difficult for us.' During the 'Battle of Hamburg', 86 aircraft were lost out of a total of 3,095 despatched (2.78%).

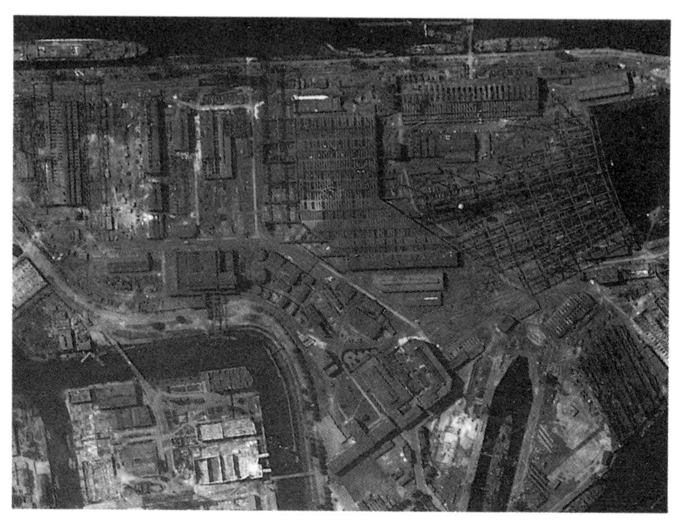

The Blohm and Voss shipbuilding yards in the Steinwarder Waltershof area, showing damage to many of the installations.

Devastation amongst oil storage areas in the docks.
(Both Imperial War Museum)

The city centre of Hamburg reduced to smoking rubble by RAF and USAF attacks in July and August 1943. (Imperial War Museum)

Dr Albert Speer said after the raids: 'Hamburg has suffered the fate Göring and Hitler had conceived for London in 1940.' The attacks had '... put the fear of God...' into him. He told Hitler that armaments production was collapsing and that six more attacks on major cities, such as Hamburg, would bring Germany's armaments production to a total halt.

The 'Battle of Hamburg' was followed four months later by the 'Battle of Berlin', which would continue until March 1944. Preliminary attacks on the city had started in August 1943, and the Battle proper commenced in November. On 3rd November 1943, Harris sent a Memorandum to Churchill asking that the highest priority be given to attacks on the German capital. He said:

> 'We can wreak (sic) on Berlin from end to end if the USA will come in on it. It will cost the Allies between 400 and 500 aircraft, but it will cost Germany the war.'

The 'Battle of Berlin' began on 18th November 1943, when 440 aircraft were despatched.

On 26th November 1943, Lord Salisbury wrote to the Secretary of State for Air, and asked him if there was a change in Government bombing policy. The reply was that there had been no change, and that the aim of the Government was the progressive dislocation and destruction of the German military, industrial and economic system. The Secretary of State went on to say:

> 'I have never pretended in the House of Commons, or elsewhere, that it is possible to reach this aim without inflicting casualties on the civilian population of Germany. But neither I, nor any responsible person in the Government, has ever gloated over the destruction of German houses. We have resisted the policy of reprisals. For example, for your confidential information, I may tell you that we were under a good deal of pressure from the Poles, a year or so ago, to undertake such reprisals. The Germans were committing atrocities against the Polish civilian population on an enormous scale, and the Poles wanted us to select towns and villages in Germany for deliberate destruction. Again, the Czechs, after the destruction of Lidice, urged that we destroy a small German village and announce that if the enemy destroyed any more Czech towns or villages, we would counter with the policy of destroying a similar number of

> German towns or villages. We refused, and kept to the principle that we would only attack military objectives.'

The reply went on to say that Berlin was the heart of the German war organisation, and the greatest single centre of its war industry. Among a number of manufacturers represented in Berlin were: Siemens, Rheintall, Henschel, Dornier, Heinkel, Focke Wulf and the Daimler Benz engine factories; furthermore, twelve great railway systems met there. It was also one of the principal centres of the German canal system, and second only to Dusseldorf as an inland water port with no fewer than nine Trans-Shipment harbours. It was, also, of course, the centre of the German Government Administration.

Those opposed to attacks on civilians were not aware at the time that Bomber Command attacks caused Germany a tremendous repair burden, and made her disperse her anti-aircraft defences far and wide. For the first time in the war Germany was forced to go on the defensive, and redirect a substantial volume of industrial output towards anti-aircraft guns and night fighters instead of bombers. Such attacks also, importantly, drew a substantial part of Germany's fighter force in the East back to defend the homeland against Bomber Command raids in the West.

After the raids on Berlin, Dr Speer was very worried, particularly when he heard that the Alkett Armaments factory had been hit and set on fire: the factory was a major producer of guns and tanks. On 29th November he wrote that the factory had been completely destroyed and that other factories were in bad shape. The accuracy of the bombers made him feel that they were being guided to their targets by spies. In six raids alone, 46 factories were destroyed and 259 damaged.

The opening of a new information room at a Bomber Command HQ unit. Left to right: Air Chief Commandant KJ Trefusis Forbes, Director WAAF; Brigadier General FL Anderson, Officer Commanding US VIII Bomber Command; Group Officer LM Crowther; Air Chief Marshal Sir Arthur Harris; Lady Harris.

Field Marshal Milch told the German people:

> 'It is absolutely essential, in the areas of the country which have been so far free of air raids, that everyone must, for every moment of the day, think of air raid precaution measures.'

From March to December 1943, the damage to the main industrial centres was greater than at any other time in the war. A total of 116,500 tons of bombs was dropped in 94 attacks on 29 industrial cities. Over 2,400,000 working man-hours were lost in industrial areas because of air attacks.

On 21st January 1944, the AOC-in-C Operations submitted a further paper on the 'Progress of the Combined Bomber Offensive against German aircraft production and towns.' Of the twenty towns in Germany defined as principal targets through having aircraft industries, ten had been attacked by Bomber Command. These controlled 94% of the total population of the twenty towns and 26.5% of their built-up area had been destroyed. Of the thirty-three important German Air Force targets, nine had been destroyed by the RAF and five by the USAF.

In February 1944, Harris responded to the media's criticism of the bombing campaign, which was mainly on Berlin. He stated that incontestable evidence from highly secret sources existed to show that the continuous and probable intensification of the offensive was regarded in the highest Nazi circles as something which, in the absence of unpredictable errors by the Allies, would certainly ensure a German defeat comparatively quickly by producing a collapse of morale as well as of production on the Home Front. The efforts of the German propaganda machine, he went on to say, to divert Allied bombing by

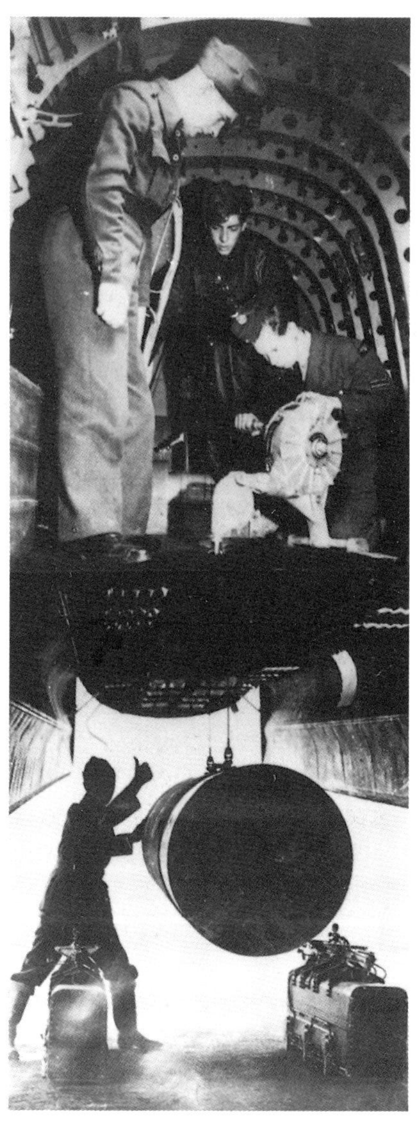

Hand-winching a 4,000 lb 'Cookie' into the belly of a 57 Squadron Lancaster at East Kirkby, 26th January 1944.

any means from industrial targets in Germany, and to convince the German people that these tactics would shortly be successful, were inconsistent with the widely and officially disseminated view that the prevalent attitude to bombing in Germany was one of apathy.

In March 1944, it was decided that the combined effects of Strategic Bombing had resulted in set-backs for the German Army on the Eastern front which had sufficiently weakened Germany to make it practical for the Allied army to invade the Continent, despite the fact that, in three operations (to Leipzig, Berlin and Nuremberg on 30/31st March 1944) 243 aircraft had been lost.

In 1943, the Germans had described attacks by Bomber Command as 'Liquidation' and in 1944 'Terror Raids', although, in fact, many Germans admitted that the attacks were aimed at industrial and armament factories within the prominent centres attacked.

In April and May, the targets were changed to German aircraft factories and, by the end of May, seventy such factories were shown by reconnaissance photographs to have been destroyed or severely damaged.

On 10th April 1944, Harris wrote to the Under Secretary of State at the Air Ministry, complaining about the statements issued to the Press by the Directorate of Public Relations. He claimed that, despite assurances by the Directorate that an improvement would be made in the standard of such reports, they remained, in his opinion, far from satisfactory. Whilst much had been made of the heavy losses incurred in two raids on Berlin and Nuremberg during March 1944, there had been no reference to the strikingly low general average of losses. His letter went on to say that the public were being given the idea that, apart from successful raids on Frankfurt, Essen and Berlin, the month of March as a whole had been a failure, whereas, in fact, it had been a great success, with outstandingly accurate attacks on factories and marshalling yards: it had also been the second best month of the war for minelaying.

German 88mm flak guns fire in unison as Allied bombers pass overhead. (Imperial War Museum)

In April 1944, Bomber Command had begun very successful attacks on railways and other targets directly connected with the success of the June landings in Normandy. Five of the most important ammunition and ordnance depots used by the German Army and Air Force in France were wrecked during May. Some 50% of the German fighter force was engaged against the Allied strategic bombing of Germany, whilst 55% of its other anti-aircraft resources were engaged in the defence of German industry. Oil plants alone were defended by some 460 guns of the 14th Flak Division.

At Juvisy and La Chappelle, two important railway centres near Paris, the whole railway complex was halted in one single attack. The Germans had hoped to get forty-eight trains per day through but, because of the bombing, the number was reduced to only six. The 9th and 10th SS Panzer Divisions had to leave their trains in the area of Nancy and travel 400 miles by road: it took them longer to reach Normandy than it had taken them to get from Poland to the Eastern Front.

From April to June, 38% of the bombs dropped were on communications centres. The Allied staff had named eighty important railway centres in France, Belgium and Western Europe which were to be attacked and put out of action. By the end of June, Bomber Command had made eighty-one attacks on railway centres, locomotive sheds, maintenance facilities and marshalling yards; and twenty-one on railway tunnels and junctions.

In the run-up to the June landings in Normandy, all attacks were concentrated on the coastal gun batteries. The night before the landings on 6th June, 5,315 tons of bombs were dropped by a thousand bombers on the ten permanent heavy coastal batteries in the area of the landings. Even if all the guns themselves were not put out of action, their ammunition was largely destroyed. To avoid identifying the exact landing area, targets were also attacked in the Pas de Calais and in Brittany.

In July 1944, Field Marshal Von Kluge was brought in to take over command of the German Army. He said that no form of strategy could counterbalance the effects of the Allied bombing, other than withdrawal from the battlefield. Field Marshal Rommel expressed exactly the same sentiments.

On 13th August 1944, Eisenhower sent a message to every Allied soldier, sailor and airman. To the RAF he said:

> 'I request every airman to make it his direct responsibility that the enemy is blasted unceasingly by day and night, and is denied safety either in fight or flight.'

In October 1944, Tedder, the Deputy Supreme Commander, wrote a paper: 'The Air Policy To Be Adopted With A View To Rapid Defeat Of Germany.' Among the targets he felt should be attacked were the following: the Ruhr, rail centres, oil targets, canal systems and centres of population.

On 7th November 1944, Dr Speer wrote to Field Marshal Keitel, saying:

> 'The continuous attacks directed by the enemy against the Ruhr are having the most serious effect on our entire armament and war production. In addition to the bombing of production plants in the Ruhr, the systematic attacks carried out on railway installations are largely responsible for the present critical situation. The following figures show the consequences of the present transport situation and reduced output.'

Coke and coal output fell in the first week of October to 273,000 metric tons, compared with 371,000 metric tons in October 1943. Steel output fell by over 300,000 metric tons, the yield for the whole Reich therefore having halved in comparison with that of the first six months of 1944. Five power stations were out of action, power supplies having dropped by 26% and gas by 50%. Ten railway stations including Essen, Hamm, Cologne and Munster were out of action in November. The waterways and canals were severely impeded by the destruction of the Muelheimer

Bridge at Cologne.

Speer went on to say that the *Führer* had ordered a thousand heavy Flak guns to be diverted from the defence of war production plants to that of communications key points. Two thousand light Flak guns were to be made available immediately for installation on railway waggons, complete with concrete cupolas to protect their crews against strafing from enemy aircraft. All armed forces and local authorities were to take all conceivable measures to restore efficiency and normality to the transport system.

On 12th December 1944, the War Cabinet produced a paper: 'The Methods of Breaking The German Will To Resist'. The object was to destroy the unity of purpose of the Nazi leaders and, consequently, the effectiveness of their control over the fighting men and the people at home; also to show the German leaders and people that 'Unconditional Surrender' was not a synonym for extermination.

In December 1944, the Germans began a counter-offensive in the Ardennes (the 'Battle of the Bulge'). Despite terrible weather conditions, Bomber Command operated during the period on fourteen nights and twice by day, attacking enemy rail communications in the general area of troop and supply concentrations vital to the success of the counter-offensive. One particular attack took place on 26th December at St Vith, which was a hub of road networks in the eastern Ardennes. German prisoners of war said later that every road was completely blocked, and that for a week after the raid a German engineer battalion was employed in restoring the roads. Two German divisions on their way to Bastogne and the defence of Vielsale were forced to by-pass the town. The delay resulted in them arriving too late to dig in and meet the Allied counter-attack. Troop concentrations were also bombed at the road junction of Houffalize.

The Americans, who had been given a severe mauling in the raid on Schweinfurt on 14th October, losing sixty aircraft out of 288 despatched (this being partly the reason for Harris not receiving complete support in attacking Berlin), later admitted to Harris that he had been right in wanting to destroy the heart of Germany - Berlin.

CHAPTER EIGHT

THE V1 and V2 ATTACKS

In 1939, it was the Committee for the Scientific Study of Air Defence, under the chairmanship of Sir Henry Tizard, which first brought to the notice of the British Government its ignorance regarding the new German weapons. It was then suggested that a scientist should be attached to the Intelligence branches of the Air Staff to find out what was wrong, and whether an improvement could be effected. The scientist selected was Dr R. V. Jones but, owing to Treasury opposition to the general proposal, war broke out before he had taken up his duties on 11th September 1939.

Eight days later, Hitler made his famous speech, 'Secret Weapon', which, in fact, made no actual mention of such a measure. However, owing to an error in the translation, some alarm was created in the UK, although it was clear from the B.B.C's recording of the speech that Hitler was not referring to a specific weapon (*waffe*) but to the *Luftwaffe* as a whole.

From the Intelligence files, Dr Jones, in a search for possible new weapons, had indications that certain weapons must be taken seriously: these included gliding bombs, pilotless aircraft, long-range guns and last, but not least, rockets. To the Naval Attaché in Oslo came an anonymous letter offering to send a report on German technical developments: acceptance could be signalled by altering the preamble to a German news broadcast on a certain evening so as to say: '*Hullo, hier ist London,*' instead of what was usually said. This was duly done and the report was received. It told Dr Jones that the Germans had two kinds of radar, that large rockets were being developed and that there was an important experimental establishment at Peenemunde, where rocket-driven glider bombs were being tested.

This was as early as November, 1939 but it was in 1943 that it became evident that experiments were being conducted in the use of new long-range weapons. The evidence was amassed by April 1943, and submitted to the Chiefs of Staff. The result was that the Prime Minister charged Mr Duncan Sandys, Joint Parliamentary Secretary to the Ministry of Supply, with the task of investigating the evidence, reporting on the form of the weapon and suggesting counter-measures. Careful and skilful interpretation of reconnaissance photographs of Peenemunde confirmed that the Germans were experimenting with long-range weapons.

Peenemunde, the experimental facility, was in the north-west corner of the Baltic: the *Luftwaffe* had built it with an airfield known as *Erprobungsytelle de Luftwaffe-Werk West* (*Luftwaffe* Test Installation), or Peenemunde West. This had become the centre for the test flying of secret aircraft, and had cost 300,000,000 gold Reichsmarks or £15,000,000 which, at today's equivalent would be in the order of £1.2 billion. It was the research station for the Army and Air Force and, in 1943, was being used to develop the V1, the flying bomb, or Doodlebug, as it became known. Later, the same facilities were used to develop and test the next generation of pilotless missiles, the V2 rockets.

It was the idea of *Generalfeldmarschal* Milch, head of the *Luftwaffe*, in the face of increased air attacks and Allied air power, to restore the strength of the *Luftwaffe* by the use of these weapons. Göring had failed in the 'Battle of Britain', but the flying bomb and the rocket could offer the means of retaliation[1].

The V1 or Fi. 103 was powered by a pulse-jet unit which Germany had been developing since 1929. Air entered the jet intake, opening, in the process, a loose shutter-like flap. At the same time low octane petrol was injected into the chamber of the motor and then ignited. The resulting explosion closed the flap, causing the hot expanding gases to be expelled from the open end of the motor, propelling the aircraft forward. As the internal pressure inside the chamber lessened, the slipstream opened the intake[2] and the cycle repeated itself. This intermittent operation of the engine gave the V1 its characteristic throbbing noise. (Trouble started for those on the ground when the motor and the throbbing noise stopped). The Argos engine used in the V1 was first tested in a glider in 1941.

The V1 first flew at Peenemunde in December 1942. It could fly at a height of three to five thousand feet at a speed of 320 to 400 mph and had a range of 250 miles. Its warhead weighed 1,870lbs when filled with RDX, and 2,031lbs when filled with Tralen.

The rocket programme in Germany was under the direction of Dr Albert Speer, the Minister for Armaments in Germany, all experiments and research being the

[1] *Retaliation. German - Vergeltungs. Hence the designations V1, V2 and V3 - Vergeltungswaffen).*

[2] *- One of the disadvantages of the pulse motor was that it had to be brought up to near cruising airspeed before there was sufficient air pressure to re-open the shutter and continue the cycle. This was achieved by the use of fixed launching ramps which quickly became targets for concentrated bombing. Some degree of mobility was achieved by dropping the V1s from Heinkel bombers already flying at the cruise speed of the bomb before it was released.*

responsibility of Dr Werner von Braun who, on 10th July 1943, was made a Professor by Hitler himself.

The Minister of Home Security in the United Kingdom, Herbert Morrison, estimated that up to 4,000 people would be killed or injured and that very heavy damage to property would be caused by the explosion of one of these bombs in London. It was he, it was said, who christened the V1 the 'flying bomb', which was also known as the 'Doodlebug'[3] and the 'buzz bomb.' It was to be fired from prepared sites in the Pas de Calais.

On 1st July 1943, a Directive was issued to Bomber Command. In order to achieve maximum surprise, an attack on Peenemunde on the heaviest possible scale was to be made as soon as the length of night and other factors permitted. A conference was held at Bomber Command HQ on 7th July, when operation orders were prepared for the attack on the three targets at Peenemunde: for security reasons, the importance of the targets was attributed to special developments relating to fighter aircraft.

Also on 7th July, in Germany, artillery *Oberst* (Colonel) Walter Dornberger[4] was summoned to Hitler's headquarters: the *Führer* wanted to be informed of the details of rocket development, and was shown film of the V2 or A4 which continued, technologically, where the V1 left off. After seeing this film he gave full permission to go ahead with the rocket programme.

[3] - *The name 'Doodlebug' owes its origins to the American service personnel stationed in England at the time.*

[4] - *Oberst Walter Dornberger - had been appointed Assistant Consultant on Rocket Development in the Waffenamt (weapons section) under Hauptmann von Horstig in 1931, and was, by 1943, in charge of all rocket development with von Braun.*

Colonel Dornberger's plan, dated April 1942, was:

1.To build and launch 5,000 V1s a year.

2.To develop special forms of artillery fire of which two types were suggested: 'Harassing' fire, to interfere with the enemy's industrial supply areas at the rear, and to upset civilian morale; consisting of battery fire of three rounds every eight minutes or grouping fire of nine rounds in eight minutes.

3.Destructive fire against industrial and communications objectives, consisting of single shot, battery, or grouped fire as above.

The code name for the attack by Bomber Command on Peenemunde was *'Hydra'*. As a full dress rehearsal, a raid was scheduled on Turin on 7th August 1943, using the 'Master Bomber' principle employed by Wing Commander Guy Gibson on the Dambuster raid three months previously. The technique involved controlling and directing the bomber force whilst it was over the target, to marshal successive waves of aircraft and to alter the pattern of attack by radio.

On 16th August 1943, Group Captain John Searby, who had been a flight commander under Gibson in 106 Squadron, had become its Officer Commanding when Gibson left to command 617 Squadron for the dams raid, and was now commanding 83 Squadron, was selected to be Master Bomber.

There were three principle targets, all roughly in line, with a convenient distance between. The method of attack was approved at a conference held by the A.O.C Pathfinder Force, Wing Commander Don Bennett, on the 17th. The plan was to attack each of the three aiming points over a period of 45 minutes, using over 500 aircraft in three separate waves. The operation was to take place on 17/18th August. At Peenemunde, there were over 4,000 engineers and workers supplemented by many slave workers from countries all over Europe, particularly Russia and Poland.

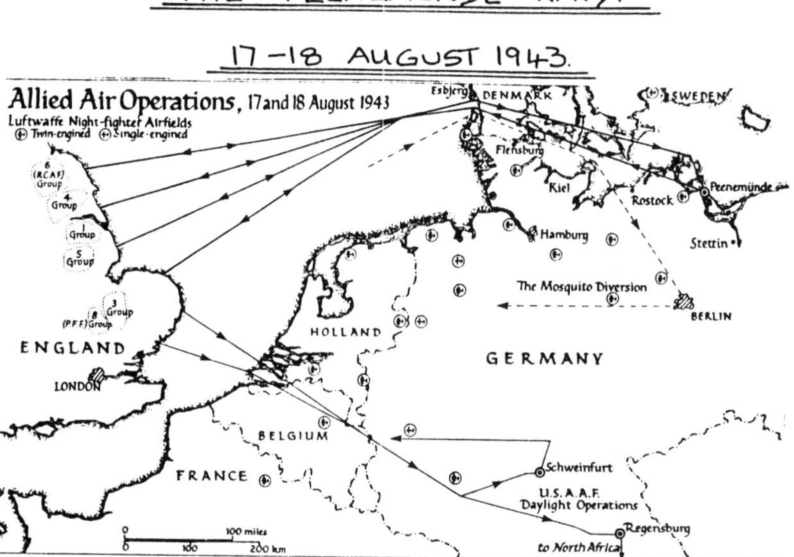

The force of 596 bombers, carrying 1,650 tons of high explosive and 274 tons of incendiaries, set out on the 600 mile trip to the Baltic. By 02.10 hrs the attack was going well, and extensive fires were seen below. At 02.45 hrs all aircraft were given the order to return to base.

A few days later photographic reconnaissance showed extensive damage to the rocket establishment. The offices of the *Nachbaudirektion Stahlknecht* were destroyed with their plans and blueprints which were required for various existing and future designs of rocket. One intended for the future was the A9, which would have had a range of 1,800 to 2,500 miles, but this had been deferred so as to concentrate on the V2 which, it was thought, would destroy London and other major cities in the UK.

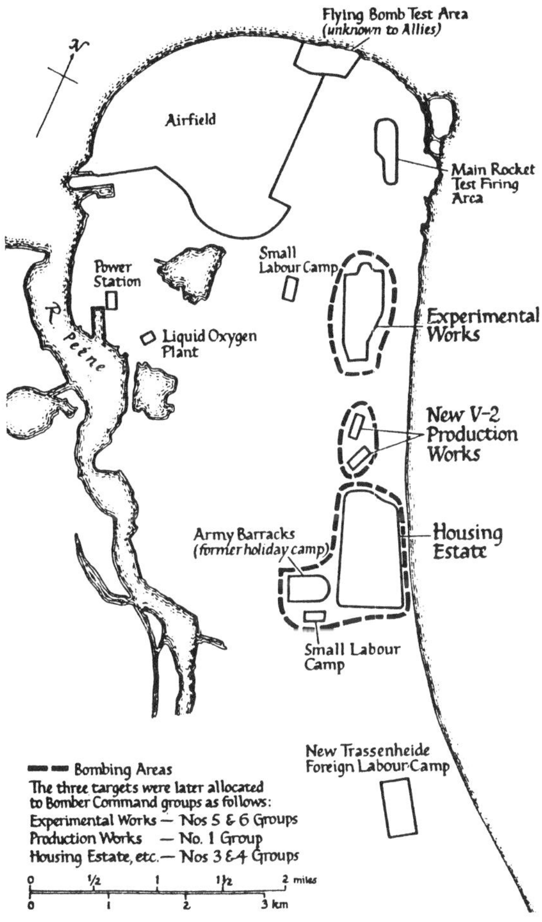

This drawing and that on preceding page by kind permission of Alan Bryett.

Among the casualties at Peenemunde was Dr Walter Thiel, the man responsible for rocket design. The attack was so severe that the Chief of the Air Staff, General Jeschonek, committed suicide the next day. The cost to Bomber Command was also high, with 41 aircraft failing to return.

In September 1943, development of the A4 (or V2) moved to a site at the Needersachswerfen in the Hartz mountains, north of Nordwaine. The rocket programme was delayed by at least two months - perhaps considerably longer - and it was April 1944 before information was received that attacks would be made on the UK by flying bombs or rockets. In June 1944, Hitler gave the order for the commencement of attacks using the V1 on England, the main target being London. On 10th June, trains were seen travelling through France carrying what looked like rockets and, from photographic reconnaissance, the Air Ministry was able to give a last-minute warning that a flying bomb attack was imminent.

The first V1 attack came on 12/13th June: flying bombs dropped in Sussex, killing six and injuring thirty. On the 15th the Germans stepped up the pressure and 200 V1s were launched, of which 73 reached London. On the 18th, the Guards' Chapel in Birdcage Walk was hit during the Sunday Service: 58 civilians and 63 servicemen were killed, and a number died later of their injuries.

In the centre of London, at the Aldwych, there were 200 casualties when a V1 dropped on 30th June. Another, shot down by anti-aircraft fire, fell on a house in Kent which was being used as a short-stay nursery. Of the 30 children there aged five or under, 22 were killed or died later: 8 of the 11 staff were also killed and those who survived were badly hurt.

The worst attack was on 28th July 1944 when a V1 fell on Woolworth's in Lewisham: 59 people were killed,

124 seriously injured and 178 slightly injured. In the first week of August 1944, 395 people were killed in London and 57 outside the capital. On the 23rd, in East Barnet, 21 people were killed.

Between June and September 1944, 8,564 V1s were launched, of which 2,419 reached the England. They left an alarming death toll of 6,184 people killed (92% of whom were in London) and 17,981 seriously injured.

A further threat arose for the people of Britain, and in particular for Londoners, in the form of the V2 or A4 rocket. Experiments on rockets had been carried out in Germany in the 1920's, and in 1934 a rocket had been fired which had reached an altitude of 8,000 feet. At Peenemunde they had begun tests with the A1 rocket, then the A2, which had reached a height of 6,000 feet. In 1938, experiments had been made with the one-ton A3 which, in 1939, was fired to a height of five miles (26,000 feet). It was a change of mind on the part of Hitler that made the A4 possible. The missile weighed 14 tons, had a one-ton warhead and a speed of 3,400 mph. It was 45 feet 10 inches long, and had a maximum body diameter of 5 feet 6 inches. It was propelled by fuel consisting of liquid oxygen and alcohol. After the power had been cut off, it commenced a dive, approaching the ground at a speed in excess of 1,700 mph and, on impact, made a crater 10 to 12 feet in diameter: however, its range was not much over 200 miles. In 1943, Hitler addressed Dornberger in the following terms:

> 'If only I had had faith in you earlier! In all my life I have owed apologies to two people only, *Generalfeldmarschal* von Brauchitsch, who repeatedly drew my attention to the importance of the development of the A4 for the future, and yourself. If we had had the A4 earlier and in

> sufficient quantities, it would have had decisive importance in the War. I didn't believe in it. Now that the long-range rocket has been developed, Europe is too small for a war. After this war is over we shall have a long period of peace, and shall be able to exploit the work done here as the leading nation in peaceful traffic among the continents.'

The plan was to attack docks, ports, installations and plants mainly in London. Operations, according to the Germans, were not intended as merely terrorising measures against the civilian population, although the German Press described them in those terms so as to bolster public morale: the term *'Vergeltung'* was applied by Goebbels. Military circles disapproved of this for security reasons, and also because they knew that hopes of the efficiency of the weapon were being raised too high. Scheduled targets were:

From the Pas de Calais:

> London, Reading ,Windsor, Brighton,
> Portsmouth, Aldershot, Chatham.

From Normandy:

> London, Southampton, Bristol,
> Salisbury, Aldershot, Chatham,
> Portsmouth, Plymouth, Cardiff, Reading,
> Windsor, Brighton.

The intended number of launched missiles was 900 per month, or 30 per day.

The first rocket was fired on Paris on 8th September 1944, killing six people. The next landed at Chiswick in London ten hours later, when three people, including a three year old girl, were killed.

The town of Antwerp in Belgium came under severe attack in October 1944, when 150 V1s and 100 V2s destroyed numerous buildings and killed many people. This continued into November, and on the 27th a V2 landed in the town, killing 159 people. In December 1944, a cinema was hit and 567 people, including 296 Allied troops, were killed.

Photograph taken from a Fleet Street roof-top showing a Flying Bomb crashing into Central London. It actually exploded in a side road off Drury Lane. (Imperial War Museum)

In England on 25th November, at New Cross in South East London, a V2 fell near Woolworth's, which at the time was full of shoppers, mainly women and children. Next door to Woolworth's was the Co-op, which was also destroyed. The total death toll was 160, plus 11 who were never seen again, and 120 injured. Two of the women missing had gone, with their babies in prams, to have tea at Woolworth's.

It was March 1945 when the last of the V1s and V2s were launched: the last V2 fell on England on 27th March in Orpington, Kent, injuring 23 people and killing one woman. A second landed on Antwerp, killing 27 people.

In Antwerp 10,145 people had been killed and injured by the V weapons. Casualties in Brussels were 238, in Liege 1,586 and in other places 2,771. The number of V2s to reach London was 517 out of 1,190 launched. Casualties there were 2,754 killed, and 6,523 injured, whilst conventional bombing raids resulted in 51,509 deaths and 61,423 injuries.

Another weapon which Germany intended to use, had she not been prevented from doing so by Allied bombing, and later the invasion, was the V3. This was an ultra long -range gun with a 400 foot barrel set in a direct line with London - a distance of 95 miles from Mimoyecques in the Pas de Calais. The shells for this gun were estimated to be of about six inches calibre, weighing about 120 lbs, with a warhead packed with some 40lbs of high explosive. The Germans could, if allowed to use this weapon, have attained a rate of fire of 25 rounds every five minutes, and double that number if the twin installation had been completed. As it was, it was totally destroyed by the bombs of 617 Squadron: the 20 foot thick concrete roof of the installation was found by the Allied armies to have collapsed, blocking the left-hand gun shaft.

When interrogated at the end of the war Göring said, on the subject of V-Weapons:

> 'You were extremely lucky that the war did not last another year or that we were unable to start to use our weapons one year earlier.'

He made further comment on the V-weapons, stating that V2 production had been held back by the ridiculous Navy programme, particularly the building of battleships, and that the original concept of the V2 had been to develop an express mail service to the US. The German Army had then sponsored further research and development. Göring was much impressed by the V2 and spoke with pride and enthusiasm when he described having seen it fired.

The flying bombs had cost 3,000 Reichsmarks each and more than 10,000 had been fired at Britain. General Koller, the *Luftwaffe* Chief of Staff said, '...the final role of the flying bomb and the A4 rocket was to replace the bomber arm of the *Luftwaffe* entirely.' Hitler had agreed with him, and the German Air Force had been allowed to decline.

Albert Speer said that, for the 10,000 flying bombs built, 3,000 fighters could have been provided. The rocket, he went on say, was too expensive to build at 15,000 Reichsmarks each.

Generalfeldmarschal Milch had told Hitler that with the defeats in North Africa and Russia, it was vital that Germany should hold off any Allied landings in the West (the so called 'Second Front'), but Hitler had insisted that, if the landings took place, a thousand rockets should be fired. He had also urged that the rocket programme and the attacks should begin no later than December 1943: as it was, this did not happen until after the Normandy landings in June 1944.

At the end of the war, the V2s found by the advancing Allied armies were shipped to the USA (together with Werner von Braun and numerous other key staff), and formed the basis of the ballistics war.

CHAPTER NINE

THE YALTA CONFERENCE

In September 1944, the Allies and the Russians began to exchange information on their own special plans for operations designed to bring the war in Europe to a close in 1945.

The general groundwork for close co-operation and assistance in the forthcoming operations was discussed. On 10th December 1944, the US Ambassador to Russia, Averill Harriman, personally stated to Marshal Stalin that General Dwight D Eisenhower, the Supreme Allied Commander, was very anxious to operate in concert with the Russians, and to help them with whatever support could be given. This included the use of Allied air forces in the Mediterranean, and in support of Russian land operations in the Balkans.

On 23rd December 1944, President Roosevelt informed Stalin that, given the Marshal's permission, General Eisenhower would be instructed to send a representative to Moscow to:

> '...discuss with you the situation in the West, and its relation to the Russian Front, in order that information essential to our efforts may be available to all of us.'

On 26th December 1944, Stalin gave his approval to the nomination of the officer designated to confer with him, Marshal of the Royal Air Force Sir Arthur Tedder, the Deputy Supreme Commander. Tedder was also immediately responsible to the Supreme Commander for all Allied air operations. Among the topics discussed by Stalin and Tedder at their meeting, which took place on 15th January 1945, was the employment of the Allied Strategic Air Forces in the forthcoming combined operations. At the meeting, Tedder outlined to Stalin the application of the Allied air effort, with particular reference to strategic bombing of communications as represented by oil targets, rail-roads and waterways. There was also specific discussion of the problem that would face the Russians if the Germans attempted to shift forces from the West to the East, and of the necessity of preventing this possibility.

On 25th January 1945, the Joint Intelligence Sub-Committee of the British War Cabinet, which was responsible for preparing such analyses for the Allied air forces, presented to Tedder, through appropriate channels, a working paper entitled:

'Strategic Bombing In Relation To
The Present Russian Offensive.'

The findings of this authoritative body were as follows:

> 'The degree of success achieved by the present Russian offensive is likely to have a decisive effect on the length of the war. We consider, therefore, that the assistance which might be given to the Russians during the next few weeks by the British and American strategic bomber

> forces justifies an urgent review of their employment to this end. It is probable that the Germans will be compelled to withdraw forces, particularly Panzer Divisions, from the Western Front to reinforce the East... To what extent air bombardment can delay the move eastwards of these or other divisions destined for the Eastern Front is... an operational matter. It is understood that far-reaching results have already been achieved in the West by the disruptive effect of Allied air attacks on marshalling yards and communications generally. These have hitherto been aimed at giving assistance to the Western Front, and should now be considered in relation to delaying the transfer of forces eastwards.'

The Russian campaign on Berlin had started between 12th and 15th January 1945 and, by 1st February, the Russians were 50 miles from the German capital.

On 25th January, Churchill contacted the Secretary of State for Air, Sir Archibald Sinclair, concerning possible attacks on Berlin and other large cities in East Germany. On 26th, Tedder had discussions with about attacks on Berlin: he then spoke to Air Marshal Bottomley, the Deputy Chief of the Air Staff, and said he was prepared to attack Berlin, and any of the three other cities named.

A note from Churchill to the Secretary of State for Air, dated 26th January read:

> 'I did not ask you last night about plans for harrying the German retreat from Breslau. On the contrary, I asked whether Berlin, and no doubt other large cities in East Germany, should not now be considered especially attractive

> targets. I am glad that this is "under examination". Pray report to me tomorrow what is going to be done.' (Initialled W.S.C)

On 27th January 1945, Portal informed Bottomley that he agreed that, after oil installations, aircraft jet engine factories and submarine building yards, all available effort should be given to attacking Berlin, Dresden, Leipzig, Chemnitz or any other city, so as to cause confusion in the evacuation from the East, and also damage morale. The bombing, however, would not begin until the Russians had crossed the River Oder in strength.

On the same day, Sinclair sent a minute to Churchill informing him that the Air Staff had made arrangements to undertake attacks on Berlin, Dresden, Chemnitz and Leipzig, or other cities in the East, to hamper the evacuation and movement of troops. This plan was given the code name 'Thunderclap'. The attacks would have to be undertaken after 4th February 1945 when, it was predicted, the moon would have waned and weather conditions improved.

On 28th January 1945, the Deputy Chief of the Air Staff consulted with the Vice Chief of Air Staff, Sir Douglas Evill, and with General Spaatz of the USAF, concerning the Russian offensive. After this, Air Marshal Bottomley flew to the S.H.A.F.E. HQ in Paris to discuss the situation with Tedder.

On 31st January 1945, the Allied decision was made to make Dresden a second priority target because it was a primary communications centre of importance to the Germans, in view of the Russian advance. This was founded on basic and explicit exchanges of information between the Allies and the Russians, and was clearly a strategic decision of mutual importance to both Powers.

TOP SECRET DSC/TS.100 TOP SECRET

SHAEF

STAFF MESSAGE CONTROL

OUTGOING MESSAGE

TOP SECRET

URGENT

TO FOR ACTION : AIR OFFICER COMMANDING, MALTA PLEASE PASS TO "CRICKET" PERSONAL FOR CHIEF OF THE AIR STAFF

FOR INFO : HEADQUARTERS, USSTAF (MAIN) FOR SPAATZ; AIR MINISTRY, WHITEHALL FOR VICE CHIEF OF THE AIR STAFF

FROM : SHAEF MAIN FROM DEPUTY CHIEF OF AIR STAFF

REF NO : S-77217 TOO: 311230A

You will wish to know that, following your talk with SPAATZ and myself and as a result of discussions with TEDDER, we have arrived at the following order of priorities for Strategic Air Forces to meet the present situation. You know, however, that these priorities will be primarily determined by weather conditions:

(A) Main synthetic oil plants continue to hold first priority for all Strategic Air Forces. They will be attacked by day whenever visual conditions are anticipated.

(B) Next in order of priority for Air Forces operating in the UNITED KINGDOM is attack of BERLIN, LEIPZIG, DRESDEN and associated cities where heavy attack will cause great confusion in civilian evacuation from the east and hamper movement of reinforcements from other fronts. SPAATZ has already ordered day attacks to be made on BELIN whenever weather conditions permit. You know the intentions of Bomber Command.

(C) Next in order of priority is attack of communications, particularly as affecting the assembly, entrainment and movement of major reinforcements to the east and as affecting current and impending land operations. For

SMC OUT 4025

TOP SECRET

- 1 -

TOP SECRET COPY NO

THE MAKING OF AN EXACT COPY OF THIS MESSAGE IS FORBIDDEN

-2-

T O P S E C R E T

REF NO: S-77217

Strategic Air Forces in UNITED KINGDOM attacks are now being directed particularly against targets in RUHR-COLOGNE-KASSEL Area. Fifteenth Air Force has been directed to pay particular attention to any signs of transfers of forces and will attack appropriate communications centres as necessary.

(D) Attack of jet targets and communications in south German Area.

Marginal effort will be directed on tank factories and submarine yards. Marginal effort on tank factories is likely to be substantial since these constitute convenient tactical "Filler" targets in areas of priority oil targets.

In addition, the priority task of the strategic day fighters after the escort of bombers is the attack of rail movement on the main routes of reinforcement to the east.

In view of the rapid Russian advance, particularly towards BERLIN, the Russians may wish to know our intentions and plans for attack of targets in eastern GERMANY. The Combined Chiefs of Staff will doubtless be considering this situation and we assume will inform SPAATZ and myself as to any limitations on the operations already ordered for USSTAF and Bomber Command.

SPAATZ asks that KUTER be informed of this signal.

ORIGINATOR : DSC (DCAS)

INFORMATION : DCOS (AIR)
SGS

AUTHENTICATION: A W TEDDER
Air Chief
Marshal

SMC OUT 4025 31 Jan 1945 1247A AGD/jos REF NO: S-77217
TOO: 311230A

T O P S E C R E T

-2-

Yalta: seated round the table (left to right) Marshal Stalin; not named; not named; Admiral Leahy (USA); Mr Stettinius; President Roosevelt; Mr Averill Harriman (US Ambassador to the USSR); Sir Alexander Cadogan (Permanent Under Secretary to the Foreign Office) and Winston Churchill. (Imperial War Museum)

On 4th February 1945, President Roosevelt, Prime Minister Churchill and Marshal Stalin, together with their Foreign Secretaries and military advisors, assembled at Yalta in the Livadia Palace, which overlooked the Black Sea. They were there to present their specific plans and requests for bringing the war to an end. At the conclusion of the presentation, General Antonov made specific requests for Allied assistance to the Russians:

1. To support the advance of the Allied troops on the Western Front, for which the situation was considered very favourable, to:

(a) defeat the Germans on the Eastern Front; (b) defeat the German groupings which had advanced into the Ardennes; (c) weaken the German forces in the West by causing them to shift their reserves to the East. It was desirable to begin the advance during the first half of February.

2. By air action on communications, to hinder the enemy carrying out the shift of his troops to the East from the Western Front, Norway and from Italy. In particular, to paralyse the junctions of Berlin and Leipzig.

It was the specific request of the Russians for the bombing of communications, coupled with the emphasis on forcing troops to shift from West to East through communication centres, that would lead to the bombing of Dresden. The structure of the Berlin-Leipzig-Dresden railway complex required that Dresden, as well as Berlin and Leipzig, be bombed.

On 6th February, General Kuter, representing General H. H. Arnold of the US Army, read a statement on behalf of the United States Chiefs of Staff, setting out their views on the matter of bombing in support of the Russian advance. The objectives, as they saw them, were:

> 1. To continue to do the greatest possible damage to the German military and economic system.
>
> 2. To avoid interference with or danger to the Soviet forces advancing from the East.

3. To do what was possible to assist the advance of the Soviet Army.

The Chief of the Air Staff, Sir Charles Portal, fully supported the proposals put forward by General Kuter, which would entirely cover British requirements. On 7th February 1945, General Spaatz informed Major General John R. Deane, Chief of the United States Military Mission, Moscow, that the communications targets for strategic bombing by the Eighth Air Force were, in order of priority, Berlin, Leipzig, Dresden, Chemnitz, and others of lesser importance.

The 'Big Three' conference: seated in front, Churchill, Roosevelt and Stalin. Behind: Field Marshal Sir Harold Alexander, Field Marshal Sir Henry Maitland Wilson, Field Marshal Sir Alan Brooke, Admiral of the Fleet Sir Alan Cunningham, Air Chief Marshal Sir Charles Portal, Admiral Leahy, General Marshal and Russian delegates.
(Imperial War Museum)

TARGET - DRESDEN

On 8th February 1945, S.H.A.E.F. (Air) informed Bomber Command and the US Strategic Air Forces that Dresden was among a number of targets which had been selected for bombing because of their importance in relation to the movements of military forces to the Eastern Front. This was based on the recommendations of the Combined Strategic Targets Committee, S.H.A.E.F. (Air) and the Joint Intelligence Committee, in keeping with the procedural structure and authority set up in S.H.A.E.F. for the conduct of aerial operations by Allied forces.

On 9th February 1945, a list of targets was fixed:

1. Berlin
2. Dresden
3. Chemnitz
4. Leipzig
5. Halle
6. Plauen
7. Dessau
8. Potsdam
9. Erfurt
10. Magdeburg

On 12th February 1945, the Russians were informed of the American intention to bomb Dresden with a force of bombers on the 13th.

CHAPTER TEN

THE PLANNING

The weather in February, particularly in the area of Dresden, was poor. The flight to Dresden would mean a nine hour flight, and the weather forecast was therefore of immense importance. With the distance involved, diversionary operations would also be important in taking fighters away from the flight path of the bomber force.

At the time Harris received the order to attack Dresden, the whole of Europe was covered in cloud but, on the 13th, the day of the attack, the meteorological staff at Bomber Command promised reasonable conditions.

The operation would be in two parts, the Americans attacking by day and Bomber Command the same night. However, during the day of the 13th, the weather was not as good as had been expected, with thick cloud and frosty snow over Dresden. This meant reversing the roles, so that Bomber Command was detailed to attack on the 13th, and the Americans on the morning of the 14th. The weather conditions would certainly favour Bomber Command, since a frontal belt was running north to south over Europe and would give cloud cover over the Ruhr and in the area to the east.

The attack by Bomber Command would be in two phases, separated by a three-hour interval[1]. The Lancaster

[1] *The three-hour separation between attacks was another crucial factor in the destruction of Dresden. Whether it was part of the plan is unclear, but the result was that after the initial attack the rescue services moved in and began work in earnest. Obviously they were completely committed to this when the second wave, dropping almost exclusively H.E bombs, arrived. By the time the bombing was over, a*

force to Dresden was to be routed directly across the Ruhr defensive belt, in what was referred to in the original reports as the 2JD and North JD areas, where it was anticipated that the ground and fighter defences would be incapacitated by the weather.

The route would then go north of Kassel and Leipzig to Dresden, with the return route home passing south of Nuremberg and Strasbourg. A Halifax force would take a direct route to attack Bohlen in anticipation that it would divert the fighter force of 7JG (sic) away from the Dresden area.

On the 13th came the Operation order instructing 5 Group of Bomber Command to despatch 230 plus aircraft to attack Dresden, and to burn and destroy an industrial centre. The marking point was a sports ground in Dresden. This would be marked with red Target Indicators (TI's) and, if assessed as accurate, would be backed up by further red TI's. The overall code name for the operation was to be *Chevin*.

At 13.30hrs, the weather over Dresden showed a chance of a break in the cloud to about 5/10 which would hold until 16.15hrs. The take-off time for the first wave was set at 18.00hrs and for the second 21.00hrs: the fuel load for each aircraft was 2,154 gallons.

The first wave would consist of 245 Lancasters and 9 Mosquitos of 5 Group, and the second wave of 529 aircraft from 1, 3, 6 and 8 Groups and 55 Squadron.

The Master Bomber's callsign was *Kingcole 1* and his deputy's *Kingcole 2,* with the overall callsign for the

huge toll had been exacted on the rescue workers and their equipment, leaving the thousands of people who were trapped without any hope of rescue. Similarly, any hope of controlling the firestorm was completely lost.

main force being *Strongman*.

The American bomber crews were detailed to attack two alternative targets: if the weather was suitable they would attempt Plan B, Dresden, where the railway yards and stations were the main target. If conditions were cloudy in Central Germany, the alternative target was to be attacked - Plan A, Kassel. However, because of the adverse weather, both Plans B and A were cancelled and the attack on Dresden was switched to Bomber Command.

At 9am on the 13th, Harris, having studied all available reports, ordered the attack on Dresden to be carried out that night. An order was sent to all Commands detailed for the attack, known as 'Laying On'. The bomb dumps on stations all over England would be told the bomb load for that night, and groundcrew would estimate the target by the amount of fuel being pumped into each aircraft. The Master Bomber's load was red target indicators plus 500lb bombs. Crews all over Lincolnshire, Yorkshire and East Anglia would not know the target until the briefing in the afternoon.

One interesting piece of Intelligence had come via Colditz Castle, thc home of officers who had, in their own way, continued to fight the war by continually escaping from other prisoner of war camps all over Germany, thereby ending up at the one from which it was said to be impossible to escape. The information had come from the German guards at the Castle, who had been asked if there were any barrage balloons over Dresden: the answer was that there were none.

Flight Lieutenant William Topper of 627 Squadron, based at Woodhall Spa in Lincolnshire, had been selected for the important task of leading the marking team of nine Mosquitos. He had joined the RAFVR in 1938 but, as he had been a newspaper journalist (at that time a reserved occupation) he was not called up for wartime service in the regular Air Force until May 1940.

At the briefing at Woodhall Spa, the Intelligence staff were unsure about the defences at Dresden: light flak was known to be sited on trains in the railway sidings around the city but, of the Sportsplatz chosen as the marking spot in the city, little was known. Thus the target maps with which crews were usually supplied were not forthcoming. However, at 54 Base, Coningsby, a montage of photographs was made up of the city centre, and circles were drawn around the marking point: to Topper, this suggested that Dresden had been added to targets listed for attack, but at very short notice.

There was some speculation about the new camera being fitted to Topper's aircraft, Mosquito DZ 631-W. On 26th January 1945, he had taken up a Mr Voller for a flight from Farnborough to test the new equipment: it was now to be used for the first time operationally, on Dresden.

The question put to the inmates of Colditz about balloons at Dresden, and the installation of the low flying camera were events which today Topper feels were related. The presence of balloons could have been a major problem.

The camera fitted in the Mosquito would take six photographs, the first as the TI's dropped, and thereafter at one second intervals, requiring the pilot to fly as straight a track as possible. Photographs had to be as sharp as possible because 5 Group wanted to know the accuracy of the marking. The pulses of the 627 crews certainly quickened when they were told they were marking for the whole of Bomber Command at Dresden that night.

The route for the Mosquitos would take them towards Chemnitz, and then they would turn sharply towards Dresden, diving as they did so. Their orders were that if any of them got into trouble they were to make all efforts to get as far back to the West as possible before abandoning their aircraft: in no circumstances were they to fly East. The callsign for the marking team was '*Platerack*' and H-Hour for the start of bombing was 22.10hrs: take-off time was 19.30hrs.

Marking was to be completed as quickly as possible, so as to be out of the way by the time the main force arrived and came in to bomb. Each of the Mosquitos carried 1 x 1,000lb Red TI.

The crews were; Topper with his navigator, Flying Officer Garth Davies; Flying Officer Walker and Warrant

Officer Oatley; Flight Lieutenant Armstrong and Pilot Officer Patterson; Flying Officer Buckley and Flight Lieutenant Crosbie; Flying Officer Rolland and Flying Officer Holling; Flight Lieutenant Alford and Flight Sergeant Murphy; Flying Officer McLellan and Flying Officer Phillips; with Flying Officer Olsen and Flying Officer Chipperfield in the last Mosquito to attack.

Wing Commander Maurice Smith was selected as Controller of the overall attack on Dresden, and was to fly in Mosquito KB 401-E with navigator Pilot Officer Leslie Page. Page's main concern was that the return trip to Dresden was very near the operational range of the Mosquito, and therefore left little room for error in navigation. They would have to fly on an almost direct line towards Chemnitz, altering course for Dresden only at the last moment. The main force would, as was usual, steer a dog-leg course to Dresden.

The charts showed no flak defence rings around Dresden but, without firm evidence, that could not be taken for granted. At briefing, crews were told that Dresden was one of the few main centres of communication between the Russian Front and Germany, and that refugees were flooding back into Dresden from Berlin.

Ron Aston was detailed to fly his first operation to Dresden as second pilot ('second Dickie') to Flying Officer Greenfield of 61 Squadron. He remembers the briefing clearly. The target in Dresden was the railway station and sidings: many trains were due to arrive from Berlin and they were to bomb so as to cause maximum havoc intended to break the morale of those left defending Berlin.

Leslie Hay (ex-49 Squadron) remembers that the attack was be to carried out in two phases: the first by 250 aircraft of 5 Group, carrying 4,000lb bombs and incendiaries to set the target alight, and the second, two hours later, by 350 aircraft carrying high explosives. The markers were to be placed in a football stadium and H hour was 22.15hrs. At H hour minus 11 minutes, Green TI's would be dropped by the use of Loran: at H Hour minus 10 minutes the first markers would go down, after which the Master Bomber would assess accuracy and, if correct, give instructions for the back-up markers to go in or, if required, to correct the marking.

The main force bombers were to be in sections, each being given a specific area of the target to bomb: and each aircraft was given a separate heading but the same aiming point, thus creating a cartwheel effect. The Intelligence Officer at briefing said that Dresden was a key city in the path of the advancing Russians. It was an old city which contained timbered houses in the centre, and was regarded by the Germans as a 'safe city'. Much of the administration had been moved there from Berlin, and many members of the High Command and other important people had sought sanctuary there from the bombing of other cities in Germany. It contained large railway marshalling yards, through which supplies were sent to the Front.

All the targets on the 'Thunderclap' Directive were important railway marshalling yards. Attacks would strangle supplies to the enemy, and shorten the war.

Flight Lieutenant John Robinson, a wireless operator/air gunner, served with 9 and 514 Squadrons and completed a tour of operations in April 1944. During this tour he had taken part in the 'Battles of Berlin and Hamburg'. Three of his crew had volunteered for a second tour with 149 Squadron at RAF Nethwold. On 9th February 1945, only four days before the attack on Dresden, Robinson received a call from his former pilot,

Squadron Leader Colin Payne DFC: he wanted Robinson to join him at Nethwold. Robinson immediately agreed and Payne flew up to where Robinson was stationed and took him back to Nethwold. On the 13th, Robinson and his crew were detailed for the operation to Dresden. On the wall of the briefing room was a large map, with the target indicated for that night. The Intelligence Officer emphasised that the target was full of German troops and equipment from the Russian Front. All his comments were directed at the military issue of the operation. It would be, for Robinson and his crew, the longest trip so far undertaken.

Peter Hoare was with 106 Squadron, and remembers the briefing and the announcement that Dresden was to be the target that night - a target with industrial and communications features. He felt that the Germans had by then lost any claims to sympathetic non-targeting. He also considered Dresden a long and deep penetration trip, with all its attendant hazards and problems. The target was shown at the briefing as being a road and railway centre of some importance.

Flying Officer John Woolams was serving with 405 Canadian Squadron, and Dresden was to be his 59th operation. He arrived at the briefing room at 17.45hrs for a briefing at 18.00hrs which lasted about an hour. 'Back-and-front bibs' were issued, on the front the Union Jack, on the back a message 'I am a British Airman'. Dresden was only 20 minutes flying time in an easterly direction from Russian-held territory, and any captain of an aircraft too badly damaged to make it back to base had the option of flying due east for as long as he could, and then baling out.

Squadron Leader Canning remembers the target within Dresden being the marshalling yards, where railway traffic and trains carrying ball-bearings for use in war machinery passed through.

A Canadian serving in 419 Canadian Squadron was Marvin Scale. He was a navigator, responsible for getting his crew to the target and back. His main concern (a common one throughout Bomber Command before Dresden) was the duration of the flight and the time spent over enemy territory. Based on past experience, the operation would mean heavy casualties for Bomber Command.

Allan McDougall was a flight engineer with 100 Squadron, and his main concern was the amount of fuel required.

Frank Pritchard arrived on 550 Squadron, from a conversion unit, on the day of the operation to Dresden. He and his crew were moved by truck from Blyth to North Killingholme, the home of 550 Squadron. When the truck stopped at the Orderly Room, the face of Flying Officer Joe Pascoe DFC RAAF appeared over the tailgate of the truck: he said he was short of a gunner for ops that night and asked for a volunteer to fill the vacancy. Frank offered to do so and was accepted.

John Whitely had joined the Territorial Army in March 1939 and later, in 1940, volunteered for aircrew in the RAF. In July 1941, he was required to report to the Aircrew Recruiting Centre which, in those days, was the Long Room at Lord's Cricket Ground, St John's Wood, London. After training, he was posted to 619 Squadron: he was told at the briefing for the Dresden raid that it was a 'virgin target' and a staging post for the German Army, and that the raid would help the Russians who were advancing from the East.

At 467 Australian Squadron, Sergeant Arthur Beer remembers the briefing as 'Tonight we go to Dresden. It is a virgin target with a population of about 600,000, which we hope will be considerably less by the morning'. In the light of day and 50 years on these seem harsh words, but the RAF had been fighting a hard and bloody battle for over five years so perhaps such sentiments then were understandable.

At 100 Squadron, there was a slightly different slant, as Kenneth John remembers. They were told they were helping the Russian advance from the East, and that the raid was also to stop Nazi officers fleeing Germany through the area of Dresden, via Czechoslovakia.

Flight Sergeant Deryck Thurman had joined the Air Training Corps in 1941, having had an interest in flying and aircraft model making. However, when he was old enough to volunteer for aircrew duties, he was rejected on medical grounds. Later, in 1943, when he again volunteered, he passed the medical and, in August 1944, passed out as a flight engineer, joining 149 Squadron in December. The briefing room was a large Nissen hut, which had a large map of Europe on the wall. Pilots, navigators and bomb aimers had attended an earlier briefing, and the remainder of the crews a later one. When Deryck's pilot emerged, the look on his face told the crew that something was up, but all he could say was: 'Wait till you see the map'. When they got inside and saw the map, there were a few intakes of breath. The coloured cotton on the map, denoting the route to the target, seemed to go on for ever.

George Futer was with 97 Squadron, whose task it was to illuminate the target for the marking Mosquito aircraft. When they arrived at the briefing room, the map on the wall was covered for security reasons. The Squadron Commander entered the room, followed by the Station Commander. The murmur went around that something big was on, particularly as 'Groupie' had turned up. He spoke first and said:

> 'Gentlemen, it is evident to us all that the war in Europe is almost over. However, we do not believe that Hitler will surrender while there is any semblance of fighting strength left in his Army. We expect him to make one last desperate stand in Germany. His forces retreating on the Eastern Front will pour back into the homeland for this final battle. Already, troops are assembling to be routed back to the home front. There is only one route his soldiers can take. It is the only intact rail network capable of handling the traffic. These German troops are assembling and awaiting transportation through Dresden. Tonight, we attack Dresden with upwards of 700 Lancasters. We intend to completely disrupt German communications with the Eastern Front. Dresden is the key to these communications. It must be destroyed.'

The briefing was then taken up by the Squadron Commander, a Wing Commander, who went on to say:

> 'German fighter strength is dwindling and you should meet no concerted opposition from that quarter. However, do not minimise the situation: the Luftwaffe still has a good many serviceable aircraft at its disposal. We assume that flak will be moderate to heavy over the target, but we have no reliable estimates as to the number of anti-aircraft guns or searchlights in the city. Some of the wireless operators will be acting as

monitors to relay radio transmissions from the Pathfinders to other 5 Group aircraft.'

The chit-chat was rather more than usual before an operation: 'Why the hell are we bombing Dresden?' and so on.

On this operation Futer's aircraft was flying as 'Emergency Marker', which meant they would be up front, following the Primary Blind Markers, but would not drop their Target Indicators unless ordered to do so by the Master Bomber, who had to decide if the bombing was correct or not. They would come around on their bombing run, and then orbit the target for the duration of the attack, or until requested to re-mark the aiming point.

Wing Commander Smith's job was controlling the markers to ensure that they were dropped in the correct spot: he then had to direct the main force if the bombs did not fall in the right place, so as to correct the situation. Before Zero Hour, the Primary Blind Markers were to drop green TI's, and then the Mosquitos would mark the target with Red TI's. If the first Red TI dropped by Topper was correct, then the remainder of the Mosquito force would back it up with further Reds. The main force would then bomb on the centre of the Red TI's. As the Russians were so close, no risk could be taken of any of the Lancasters going astray and bombing the Russian lines. This was the main reason for using Loran on the Dresden raid. The Loran sets were installed in the Mosquitos which would control and mark the target. If they got it right, there was every chance that the main force would bomb on the correct spot.

The other target on the 13th was the Bothlen oil refinery which was to be attacked at 22.00hrs, 15 minutes before the attack on Dresden began. This operation was to be carried out by Halifax squadrons, the Lancaster squadrons attacking Dresden.

In the early part of the war, 250lb bombs had been dropped. Now the bombs were 4,000 and 8,000lb 'Cookies', one of which alone could demolish a city block: if this were multiplied by 700, it would mean the end of an entire city.

All that was left was for the crews to board the aircraft, and set out for the long haul to Dresden.

CHAPTER ELEVEN

TARGET - DRESDEN

Bombing was a precise and specialist operation. All bomb aimers were well trained, and the majority vowed to do their best to drop their loads on the selected targets. Weather conditions, of course, played an important part in this, and were often found not to be as forecast in pre-operation briefings.

Les O'Hanlon's crew were 'press-on' types: the bomb aimer, Flight Lieutenant Nicoll, would always instruct his skipper to go around again if conditions were not right, or if, for one reason or another, he was put off at the moment of dropping the bombs. The run-up to the target was crucial, the pilot having to keep the aircraft on a straight and level run despite flak defences and enemy fighters in the target area. The whole purpose of the operation hinged on that short period which, to the crews, seemed a lifetime - running in to the target. To have to go round again for any reason was, as Les described it, '...like tearing your guts apart.' But, as a crew, at the beginning of their tour of operations, they had agreed they would not fly to a target simply to drop their bombs anywhere and then return as quickly as possible: there had to be more to it - particularly when their lives were at stake. A fight for freedom was also at stake and the only way it could be won, and the war stopped, was to make sure that as much damage and disruption as possible was inflicted on the enemy's war effort. From then on, they went on each operation with the intention of hitting the aiming point in the target area.

Flight Lieutenant William Topper, in Mosquito DZ 631-W with Flight Lieutenant Garth Davies, his navigator, took off at 19.57hrs on the evening of 13th February 1945,

Flight Lieutenant William Topper and Flight Lieutenant Garth Davies, his navigator, in front of their Mosquito.

a date that would live on in the history of World War II when many others had long been forgotten. The Master Bomber, Wing Commander Maurice Smith, with his navigator, Pilot Officer Leslie Page, was taking off at the same time from Coningsby: Topper was based at Woodhall Spa. Both stations were in Lincolnshire, which was then, and still is, known as 'Bomber Country'. Topper climbed to 30,000 feet and headed for Chemnitz: before arriving there, however, he would alter course quickly and head for Dresden, where his vital job was to mark the aiming point for the first wave of the main force to attack. At 5,000 feet he called the controller to say he was clear of cloud, having earlier requested checks on both weather conditions ovcr Dresden and on radio reception. From then on, the conversation between the controlling aircraft was recorded

TARGET - DRESDEN

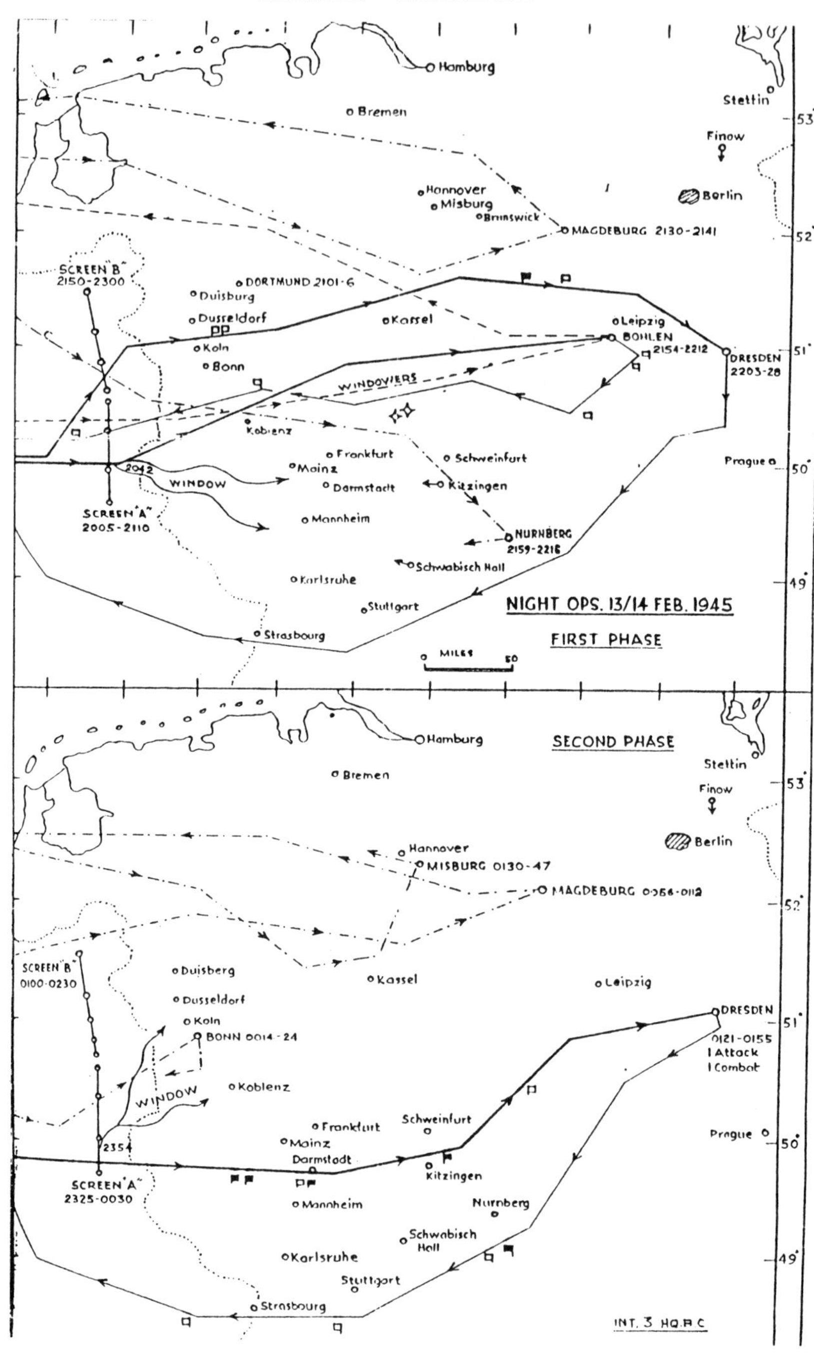

'Time to climb aboard.' Late Night Striking Force (PFF)
8 Group Bomber Command, 1945.
(F/Lt. DW Skillman, 139 Squadron)

on wire tape by the Link 1 aircraft from 97 Squadron, flown by Flight Lieutenant McConnell. His task was to communicate, in Morse, the instructions of the Master Bomber, Wing Commander Smith, to the main force should the speech transmission equipment fail or be jammed. He would also act as a communicator between the Master Bomber and Group at base in England.

The primary blind markers were dropped by 83 Squadron and, as Davies told Topper to turn to port, the flares suddenly fused at 5,000 feet above them: below, clear as moonlight, was the city of Dresden, grey and cold looking with a slight smoke pall. There ahead were the sports stadium, the main marshalling yards and the river. By this time Topper was down to 3,000 feet. The Master Bomber asked: 'Do you see the green yet?' and he replied: 'OK, I see it.' It was now up to the eight Mosquito markers to do their stuff. Topper called: 'Tally Ho!' at 22.05hrs, the usual practice to warn other aircraft that Marker 1 was about to make his run on the target. He turned in towards the centre stadium, and Davies opened the bomb doors on the Mosquito, having already selected the bomb switches. He called out each hundred feet as the altimeter unwound. At seven hundred Topper pressed the button, and away went the Red 1,000lb TI (Target Indicator). Immediately, there was a brilliant flash under the aircraft, the first photo flash going off, and they were now down to four hundred feet and levelling out, counting the flashes as they did so. Five, six and then up with the nose and full power to regain height quickly.

There was no flak, and the city seemed undefended. The controller called up: 'Hello, Marker Leader, your marker dropped about one hundred yards to the east of the marking point.' Back-up was then called for.

The Marker 2 aircraft, Mosquito 599-F, came in to continue the marking at 22.06hrs, followed in turn by the remaining six: Flying Officer Chipperfield in KB 406-Y was the last to mark the aiming point. He heard the Master Bomber tell him to hurry up and complete the marking and then clear the target area. The red splashes soon spread as more aircraft marked the target. The Main Force then started to make its run up to bomb the target area. The order PLATERACK came from the Master Bomber at 22.11hrs.

Of the 254 aircraft of 5 Group detailed to attack Dresden, 244 were successful. Topper was asked to hang around for a while by the Master Bomber, and to keep one yellow target indicator available. The remainder of the marking team were given permission to return to base. The one yellow TI held in reserve by Topper was to be used if the bombing started to creep away from the marking point out into the country. He made a number of runs over Dresden, which reminded him, from the air, of Herefordshire and Shropshire. As he climbed higher there was a brilliant blue flash, which he thought was probably a power station exploding. Shortly after this he was also given permission to depart for base. As he climbed, he entered thick cloud, but at 30,000 feet he found the stars above him. With a three hour flight back to base, the round-trip took six hours in all. He landed at 01.53hrs on the 14th. His bombing photograph, taken from eight hundred feet, was remarkable, and showed the Friedrichstadt Sportsplatz, the main aiming point.

At the end of the first attack, the controller sent a message to Platerack Force: 'Go home now, Go home'. The time was 2220. Down below, in Dresden there was confusion since, despite the bombing, people still had not been told to take cover in the shelters, it was 2209 before they were told to do so (times shown as written in official reports).

Bill Spence was flying with 44 Squadron, and was in one of the first aircraft of Platerack Force to bomb after the marking had prepared the way. His recalls the first anti-aircraft defences not being heavy, although there was some fighter activity. One fighter spotted them, and came in to attack but, when in range, it broke off without firing, and disappeared. Either it had run out of ammunition, or the pilot was a veteran. A new, inexperienced pilot would probably have pressed home his attack, while a seasoned campaigner would have realised that the blaze of Dresden behind him would make him clearly visible to the bomber's gunners, and would have deemed it better to live to fight another day.

John Whiteley of 619 Squadron was also in the first wave, and approached Dresden on a south-easterly heading. It was a dark night, with no moon or cloud, and he was able to pick up the River Elbe, which passed through Dresden from the north-west to the south-east, and bomb from 17,000 feet. He, also, was surprised at the lack of searchlights and flak defences. Having bombed the target, and viewed the area, he thought: 'We have hit the jackpot'.

John de Bell Hunt was flying in the same crew, having completed 21 operations, and remembers that, when they arrived over Dresden, the Master Bomber was circling the target and 'Wanganui' red and green markers were going down on parachutes, lighting up the target. They were given instructions to bomb, and Hunt (the bomb aimer) got on with his task: the bombs dropped, they then flew on a straight and level course to obtain a bombing photograph and headed home. As they did so the rear gunner, Bill Adams, shouted that the target was ablaze, and that there was a large hole in the cloud caused by the fires.

John Wymark was flying with 106 Squadron as a navigator, and soon found the winds to be much stronger than forecast: he informed the bomb aimer, who adjusted his sights accordingly. Some bombs were observed to be falling short, and the Master Bomber instructed Wymark's aircraft to mark ahead of the markers: this they did, and then circled to drop their bomb load. The strong wind was causing the incendiaries to fall short since (unlike high explosive bombs) they were not aerodynamic and therefore tended to spin and fall behind. With the strong north winds the fires soon spread, beginning to produce the conditions which would result in the phenomenon known as a 'firestorm.'

Angus Belford of 463 (RAAF) Squadron bombed at

H plus One. At H minus nine the Master Bomber, using Loran (similar to Gee, but with a range of 1,400 miles) had released the primary blind green parachute flare in the general area of the target. This allowed the illuminating Lancasters to adopt their planned spacing for the flare drop. The first group flew through the target area from north to south, each dropping fourteen flares at seven-second intervals. They were followed by a second group, flying west to east, with more flares. The hundred or more flares hanging on their parachutes provided artificial daylight over a wide area. To protect these aircraft from individual detection and possible destruction by flak, selected senior aircrews from various squadrons in 5 Group supported the Pathfinders from H minus twelve until the attack began. To prevent the target indicators being obliterated by their own bombs, they used a 'vectral wind' device which placed the bombs 200 metres to the left of the aiming point.

George Futer flew almost at will across Germany. Gone were the hordes of German fighters, the terrible flak barrages and the searchlights. Futer thought about Göring's boast that 'no bomber would penetrate the Reich.' It was, to say the least, a little unnerving since, in the past, just when lack of opposition had lulled them into a sense of false security, a German nightfighter would suddenly appear and attack them as they left the target area.

When they arrived, the target indicators were going down, strings of parachute-equipped flares dropped by the Pathfinders of 5 Group lighting up the target area. The bomb aimer was calling: 'Steady, steady, left left'; and then the magic words the rest of the crew wanted to hear: 'Bombs gone, all clear skipper, bomb doors closed.'

On the 5 Group Lancasters, all the armour plating which backed the guns in the turret as they were elevated had been removed, and the perspex behind the guns, extending almost to the top of the turret, cut away: this left the gunner exposed to the weather, but did improve his visibility immensely. A hundred miles away George Futer, from his rear turret, could see sheets of flame billowing high into the night air.

For George Reid, a navigator, the day of the Dresden operation was one of the most worrying of his life. His squadron (No. 50) was tasked with following the Pathfinder aircraft dropping 'Window'. From the Ruhr, his navigation instruments were jammed, and he therefore had to use 'dead reckoning' - on a pitch black night. This, he remembers, meant a lot of finger crossing. On the last leg, Reid asked the bomb aimer if he had seen anything, but the reply was: 'Nothing - just the blackness of the night.' With only five minutes to go, he again asked the same question, and got the same reply.

This went on until, according to Reid's calculations, they should have been over Dresden. Their instructions were to fly for one minute through the target area, and then turn off at a 90 degree angle to port, circle, and then come in as the last wave to bomb. As the order was given to the pilot to turn to port, the rear gunner called: 'Flare dead astern'. For any navigator, but for Reid in particular, these were sweet words, as the Pathfinders were due one minute after they had passed the target area. In his crew at the time were two Scots, two Australians and three Englishmen.

Flight Lieutenant Freddie Hullance's rear gunner, Sergeant Phil May, reported on the intercom, shortly after bombing, that the fires in the target area were spectacular and greater than anything he had previously seen. Hullance was keeping his eyes on the instruments, however, and did not allow his attention to be distracted for a quick look.

Richard Thomas was serving with 171 Squadron, part of 100 Group. He and his crew had a different role on

13th February 1945. He was flying Halifax NA 108-X, and the entry in his log reads: 'Special Operation number one and a half route Liege and Tilburg'. He took off at 18.01hrs and began, forty minutes later, to fly his 'race course.' Two wireless operators jammed the German early warning radar system for five hours with special Mandrel equipment fitted in the aircraft. They landed back at base at 00.45hrs having flown at 17,500 feet for five hours on a set 'race course pattern', turning every ten minutes.

Squadron Leader Bob Davies was also serving with 100 Group, flying B17 Flying Fortress aircraft of 214 Squadron from RAF Oulton. The flight to Dresden was quite uneventful, and it was clear over the target. Orbiting approximately 20 miles south of Dresden, he and his crew had a grandstand view of the city burning. The column of smoke he described as being like an atomic bomb explosion, although, of course, he had not seen one at the time. The column went higher than the altitude at which they were flying, which was about 22,000 feet. It was so spectacular that he called to the rest of his crew to look, including the two special wireless operators who were doing the same job as those of 171 Squadron. His main worry was whether they had enough fuel to get back: when he saw lights below, he became uneasy and the navigator endorsed his worry by saying that they were over Switzerland, having discovered that the winds, instead of being north-west at 40 knots were, in fact, at 120 knots.

On the advice of the flight engineer, Davies reduced engine revolutions to the minimum and flew for endurance, the last two hours being rather tense. Getting back to Oulton was out of the question, and he headed for the emergency runway at Manston in Kent. On successfully landing, the flight engineer estimated that they had about ten to fifteen minutes fuel left. Their problems were not over, however, as when they started engines the next day to fly back to Oulton, only three fired-up and the fourth required a starter change. Another aircraft came down from Oulton to take them back.

Wing Commander Smith was now preparing to set course for home, and his navigator was working out the route. He called up the Link 1 aircraft to report that, as far as he could see, the operation had been a success. The Link aircraft in turn radioed back to base and this message went straight to Cochrane. It was the first time Smith had relied solely on Loran as a navigational aid, the last Gee fix having left them 150 miles short of the target. It worked perfectly, and they arrived in the target area on time. His navigator was a little worried at having to rely solely on this method, and not having Gee to double-check his position.

Things were now all set for the second wave attack, three hours after the first. At about the time that the first wave was attacking Dresden, the second was taking off. This second attack was timed for 01.30hrs. Of 551 aircraft despatched, 529 successfully attacked the primary target, Dresden. The marking for the second wave was undertaken by 8 Group, Pathfinder Force.

The Master Bomber, Squadron Leader C P C De Wesselow, and his deputy, Wing Commander H J F Le Good, were both from 635 Squadron. Le Good took off first, at 22.50hrs, and De Wesselow at 22.02. When they arrived over Dresden, the target was well ablaze, the fires making it impossible to identify the aiming points. At 01.20hrs De Wesselow called for flares, and again at 01.26: at 01.27 he called for TI's and one minute later the Green TI's began to fall. They fell about a thousand yards south-west of the aiming point, and at 01.29hrs aircraft were instructed to overshoot the Green TI's by two seconds. At 01.32hrs Le Good reported Red TI's on the south bank of the river. At 01.33hrs the Main Force went

ECRET
13 STAFF (INT P.I.)
Q.B.C.

PLOT OF H2S. PHOTOGRAPHS. Nº 30.
TAKEN 13/14 FEBRUARY 1945
TARGET:- DRESDEN (1ST ATTACK)
SCALE:- 1:63,360

GROUP SYMBOL	No OF A/C REPORTING ATTACK	No. OF A/C FITTED WITH H2S CAMERAS	No OF H2S CAMERAS USED	RESULTS RECEIVED	PLOTTED	UNPLOTTED	UNPLOTTABLE
◇ 5 GROUP MARKER A/C.	234	17	14	14	6	6	2

N.B THE SECOND FIGURE IN THE SYMBOL INDICATES THE NUMBER OF SECONDS BEFORE OR AFTER THE R/P

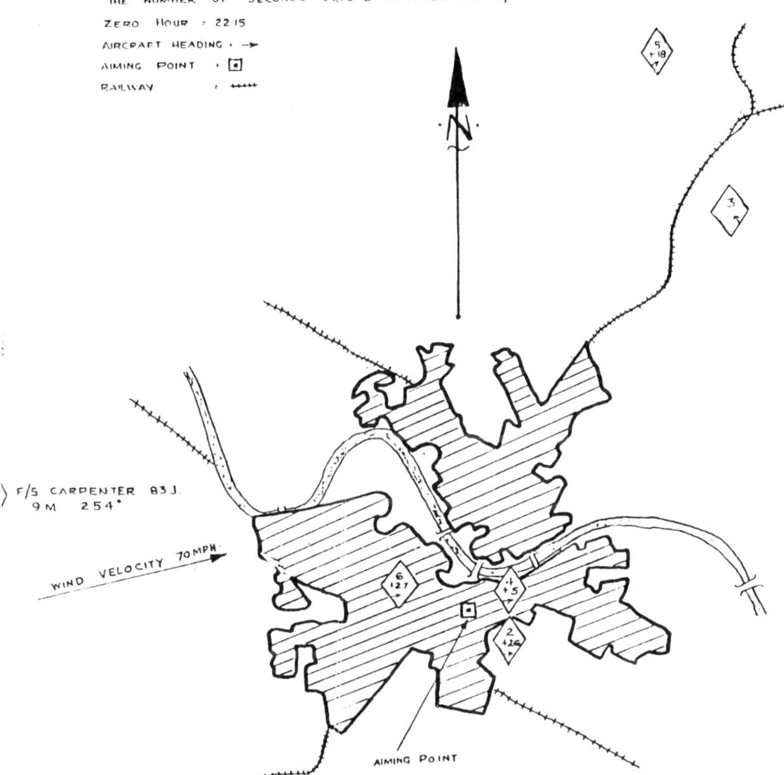

in to bomb the centre of the fires, and Le Good reported the centre of the town gutted but the marshalling yards to the south-east having escaped severe damage.

The second attack was routed across the Mainz-Mannheim defence belt, relying on the cloud to deflect the flak and anticipating that the German fighters would have been exhausted from the first wave attack. Near Luxembourg, a 'Window' force broke away from the Main Force and flew north-east in the direction of Bonn: this was in order to lure away any fighters in the area. A second Mandrel force screen was used to cover the early approaches, and the plan was successful. The Germans reported a formation of eight four-engined bombers, and it was not until they were within a hundred miles of Dresden that their real strength was realised. Despite this, no organised fighter defence was put up by the enemy, only a few being met on the outward journey, near Darmstadt, and again in the target area. They had been drawn from 1 *Gruppe* based in the area of Berlin.

From their turrets, the gunners could see a tremendous glow twenty miles from Dresden, as well as the guns of the fighting armies along the battlefield to the East. A terrific barrage was put up by the hard-pressed German forces along the River Neuess front. One Canadian bomb aimer, from Toronto, remarked: 'They won't be making china there for some time.'

The nightfighters of 4 *Gruppe* in the Frankfurt/Stuttgart area were directed against the 'Spoof' raids further north, fighter controllers being heard on several frequencies.

John Noble had come to Dresden in 1938, his father (a German) having lived in the USA for many years before returning just before World War II. He owned a camera business in the city. Down the road from his factory was one of Germany's biggest defence plants, which was still in full production up to the time of the attack. He had told his son that, despite the rumours of Dresden being an 'open city', it would be attacked. John can still remember the air trembling and the street vibrating from the roar of the Lancaster engines above. Today, he firmly believes that the attack helped to shorten the war.

Margaret Fryer, who was also in Dresden at the time of the attack, heard the sirens and the radio announcing that several bombers were approaching the city.

Squadron Leader Les Powell, of the Royal Canadian Air Force, reported to the BBC and CBC that, when the bombers left the target, it was a mass of flames, with both sides of the river saturated with fire and the glare in the sky being seen all the way out of Germany. It must have been a demoralising experience for German troops fighting on the ground against the Russian advance, a hopeless battle along the River Neuess, to see the mounting flames behind their backs.

Richard Jervis took off at 22.52hrs. Three squadrons had been asked to supply a navigator to relay for bombers under the code name 'Fire Pump', and Richard was chosen as Fire Pump Two: they were to use H2S solely on the return trip, and take photographs (with a special Leica camera) of the H2S screen.

Flight Sergeant Fearn maintains that the target in Dresden was the Zeiss Ikon AG factory, which had switched from making cameras to manufacturing bomb sights, submarine periscopes and other such precision military equipment. He also remembers selected navigators being handed a 35 mm camera fitted with a close-up lens, and being instructed to take a series of photographs of the H2S screen during the bombing, with one picture at the moment the bombs were released: he presumed this was to check the accuracy of navigation and final bombing. The camera was a Zeiss Ikon 35 mm Contax - ironically taking pictures of the destruction of its birthplace.

Flight Lieutenant Geoff Dury, a pilot with 150 Squadron, was flying Lancaster F, from 'A' Flight, on a trip he would never forget. On the bombing run, the most crucial part of any operation, the bomb aimer noticed that the master bomb switch was in the 'off' position. As a result, they had to go round three times in all before the bombs were finally released. Because of the lost time, they ended up being the last aircraft over the target below, which was a mass of flames: they were alone - apart from a Ju 88 German fighter above them. However, it took no notice of them and they, in their great wisdom, did nothing to alter that. Dury's log book recorded a trip of ten hours from take-off to landing: when they landed back at Hemswell, his legs had become locked around the middle bar of the control column, and he had to be carried out of the aircraft.

For Eddie Turner, the trip to Dresden was to have been the last operation of his tour, but the rules at about that time were changed to extend a tour from 30 to 36 operations, so he had another six to complete. To say he and his crew were a little despondent would be an understatement. Two factors contributed to this. Firstly, they had adopted Lancaster J-Jig, whose groundcrew said that crews adopting aircraft with this letter were unlikely to survive a tour of operations: to 550 Squadron it was a jinxed aircraft. Also, they had to face the fact that only eight crews had completed a tour of operations: ten had failed to return and were later reported as lost. They took off for Dresden at 22.00hrs, returning to base at 07.00hrs on the 14th. They had bombed the target at 01.30hrs from 19,000 feet. One aircraft of 550 Squadron was lost on take-off after colliding with an aircraft from another squadron: both crews were killed. Turner's recollection is that aircraft seemed to be going in all directions - amongst them the odd fighter.

Sergeant Taylor, a wireless operator who flew to Dresden with 218 Squadron, was based at Methwold. He had never seen a sight like the one he saw whilst over Dresden, a vast conflagration and all the colours of the rainbow. The flames were enormous. He and his crew were thinking the same thing, namely, that if they had to bale out, they would be lynched on the ground. On leaving the target area, both outer engines lost power; they would not feather and the propellers were just windmilling around. They began to lose height, and the pilot, Warrant Officer McCleeland, soon realised he would not make it back home and decided to make for Juvincourt in France. Sergeant Taylor reported to base that they were diverting. He also contacted the DF station at Juvincourt, receiving a bearing and course to steer, and it was there that they finally made a forced landing.

Squadron Leader Butters was a pilot with 7 (Pathfinder) Squadron: to him, Dresden was another town just like Nuremberg, Hanover and Munich. In his opinion the German war machine was evil, an affront to civilisation, and every effort had to be directed towards its defeat. He considered it legitimate to bomb all targets, towns, cities and areas of industry which prolonged the German ability to wage war.

The thoughts of some of the crews were that the civilian population would have heeded the air raid sirens, and taken to the shelters, as had the people of Coventry, Southampton, Liverpool, Plymouth and, of course, London, when they in turn had been bombed.

Marvin Seale was a navigator, and rarely looked out from his curtained-off crew position but, on this occasion, he was called to look at the target by his pilot. The return flight was particularly trying for Seale, the changes of route and altitude, and the lack of verified fixes, requiring considerable judgement to maintain track. It was a great relief to come within Gee range and find himself within 20 miles of track. They were diverted to Sudbury, and did not return to their own base until the following day.

Allan McDougal was a flight engineer with 100 Squadron, based at Waltham, near Grimsby in Humberside. He took off at 21.40hrs in Lancaster S for Sugar. It was his eighth operation. His aircraft was in the third wave to bomb, by which time the target was well lit with fires all over the city. As they came into the bombing area, they felt they were clearly in view from the fires below. As they left, the cockpit was so well illuminated from the fires that they could have read a newspaper: the fires could still be seen from the rear cockpit when they were 200 miles from Dresden. The return journey was a cat-and-mouse affair with two fighters. If an enemy fighter came into attack, he would know from any evasive action taken by the bomber that he had been spotted by his prey: the fighter which was *not* seen was the one which made the 'kill'. Because of fuel shortage they landed at Bungay after a flight of 9 hours and 40 minutes, completing the journey to base next day. McDougal refuses to go along with the idea that enemy defences became easier after D-Day.

As the Germans retreated, so their defences became more compact and precise, as was borne out by bomber losses right up to the end of the war.

Bill Austin-Clarke completed 35 operations with 90 Squadron, having joined the RAF in 1940. Over Dresden it was like daylight and, as he looked down on a residential area, he could see streets lined with trees, reminding him of a street in which he had once lived. He had taken off at 21.32hrs and arrived back at 06.57 next morning.

Kenneth Gooch was on his 51st operation, having enlisted in May and flown the majority of his operations with 35 Squadron, one of the first (if not *the* first) Pathfinder Squadrons formed in 1942. As he circled around the target, it looked to him like a cauldron of boiling tar.

Ken Brookin remembers that there were only two anti-aircraft guns at Dresden, one at each end of the city. He had been an ambulance driver in Birmingham and Coventry before joining the RAF, and had seen the German Blitz on Britain at first hand. The only dead he had seen were ARP, Rescue, Police, Fire and Ambulance personnel.

In Coventry, factories were destroyed, but, in the main, it had been private homes and the Cathedral in the centre of the City which had borne the brunt of the bombing. In Birmingham, the whole city centre had been destroyed: there were no factories there, only shops, theatres, cinemas, the Bull Ring and its associated markets, churches and civilian homes.

In Brookin's crew was air gunner Freddie Brown, who remembers that theirs was the reserve aircraft on this occasion, standing in for an aircraft which had aborted because of an unserviceable mid upper turret. His squadron, 101, despatched 21 aircraft, a maximum effort: they carried 'ABC' special operators whose role was to confuse the enemy defences and fighter controllers, one major requirement of the operator being to understand and speak German. When they arrived over Dresden, it was well alight and they were in smoke at the bombing height of 17,000 feet. When they arrived back at their base at Ludford Magna, Brown had a white ring round his mouth from wearing his oxygen mask for so long. They had seen the fires in Dresden from a distance of 120 miles, so the Russians, who were only 70 miles away, must have had a grandstand view of the attack and its effect.

Deryck Thurman took off at exactly 21.00hrs. For him, the trip to Dresden was just another operation: suddenly, the bomb aimer, who was down in the nose of the aircraft, came up and told the navigator to relax as he could see the glow of the target from what he called the

'Lincolnshire Poacher'. One of Thurman's jobs was to sit on the front end of the bomb bay and eject 'Window' through a small hole low down on the starboard side of the nose. On landing back at base at 06.00hrs the fresh air felt good after nine hours on oxygen. The whole area they had left was a sea of flames, with the streets showing black like the lines on a chess board.

Ray Base was flying with 115 Squadron from Witchford, and remembers areas of Europe covered in snow: on the way back to the UK, the headwinds were so strong that the ground speed was reduced to 80mph over France to lessen the effect of the wind. On landing back at base most of the remaining fuel was used in the circuit, and all four low fuel warning lights came on. The next day, all four engines cut out three minutes after warming up. Another 115 Squadron aircraft had to be towed to dispersal after landing, having exhausted all its fuel.

Frank Pritchard, who had only arrived on 550 Squadron on the day of the Dresden raid, was immediately asked to stand in, as one crew was a man short. He found, however, that the rear turret, which he was expected to occupy for nearly ten hours, was littered with spent cartridges and that the bulb in the gun-sight was not working; in fact, it did not even have a bulb! He told the pilot that he was unable to aim the guns without a fully working sight, and clambered out of the aircraft. When he approached the rear turret of another Lancaster in the adjoining dispersal, he had to put over a strong case to the gunner to let him have one of his three sound bulbs.

Eric Wilkin had completed a tour with 115, and was now with 7 (Pathfinder) Squadron. When they arrived over Dresden, the place was a sea of fire, and they had no trouble in seeing the aiming point, which had been so accurately marked by 5 Group three hours previously.

Joe Williams, of 625 Squadron, was on his 16th

operation, and was very surprised at the lack of opposition. Usually when they went into the target on a bombing run, they were met by thousands of rounds of blue-white explosions from 88mm anti-aircraft shells but, this time, there was only a single burst from a 105 mm shell firing with a deeper yellow-red and momentary after-glow. When Williams looked below, he saw a mass of flames: the streets stood out as dark lines which criss-crossed the area. At 01.35hrs exactly the message: 'Bombs gone, bomb doors closed' came, followed by: 'Let's get to hell out of here', but when the bomb-aimer, Flying Officer Floyd Chapman, shone his Aldis lamp through the two circular windows behind him into the thirty-three foot bomb bay, he saw that the 4,000lb 'cookie' had hung up, and was still in the aircraft. The pilot, Jim Alexander, said they would drop it on the way out, but Williams chipped in and uttered the words no crew wants to hear: 'Let's go around again, there's no flak.' The pilot replied: 'No, we will drop it.' From the tail, Williams repeated his previous plea: 'Look, there's no flak, we've brought it all this way, let's go around again. For the first and only time, Alexander told Williams to shut up.

At the briefings, crews had been lectured about the undesirability of jettisoning incendiary bombs on the way out of a target area, as inevitably a trail of fire on the ground indicated the direction in which the bombers were leaving. But out in the open country, over which they were now flying, perhaps they would not have the same effect. The bomb doors were closed by the wireless operator, Wyn Morgan, and he lifted a small plate beside his position which covered the manual release lever of number 13 bomb slip. By pulling this lever backwards, he jettisoned the 4,000lb bomb, and the bomb doors were closed. Chapman then checked with his lamp to make sure that, this time, the bomb really had left the aircraft.

Williams saw it explode, and then a great fire erupted, indicating that by sheer chance they had hit something very combustible. At 180 miles distance from Dresden, there was a semi-glow in the sky, separated by a distinct gap to the right. At the time, Williams felt that their bomb may have fallen on a village - possibly Dippoldiswalde, Altonberg, Zinnwald, or even Teplice: he hopes today that, in fact, their bomb dropped on a military target.

Reg Small and crew in front of Lancaster SR-D
Left to right: P/O Rowland, WOP; Sgt Gorman, F/Eng; F/Lt Rodgers, (Captain); F/Sgt Newman, Nav; F/Sgt Small, rear gunner; F/Sgt Mason, bomb aimer; Sgt Calvert, mid/upper gunner. (Reg Small)

Reg Small was with 101 Squadron, and remembers today how cold it was on 13th February 1945. Outside the aircraft it was 32-36 degrees below freezing, and the condensation inside his oxygen mask kept freezing in the supply tube: it had to be disconnected on a number of occasions to remove ice forming inside and blocking off the oxygen supply. His main concern, however, was the breech blocks on the guns, which were also freezing up. On the approach to the target, the pilot, Flight Lieutenant Rodgers, told the rest of the crew over the intercom that he could see very large fires ahead and, when they arrived over the target, Small saw a sight he would never forget.

Also in 101 was navigator Jack Holden. He remembers that the headwinds reached 100mph en route and that his aircraft bombed the target at 01.41hrs from 19,000 feet - one of the last to bomb in the second wave. The high winds fanned the flames to create a firestorm, as had happened two years before in Hamburg but, on this occasion, in even greater proportions. (It was claimed that the winds in the target area reached up to 400mph at ground level as huge volumes of air were drawn in to feed the flames.) The high level winds which had helped to fan the fires below had pushed them too far south of the planned route, and they were unable to fix their position until within Gee range. Consequently, they were one hour overdue at base on the return trip, having had to reduce speed to conserve fuel. The flight took 10 hours and 24 minutes.

All ABC aircraft had a crew of eight, one more than the normal Lancaster crew, the special operator being the extra member.

Flying with a Canadian squadron (405) was John Woolams, who had completed one tour on Wellingtons with 37 Squadron in the Middle East. The trip to Dresden was his 59th, and he was now near the end of his second tour. They took off at 22.19hrs, and made an uneventful trip to Dresden: they were carrying airborne target indicators, and were instructed by Squadron Leader De Wesselow to back up the TI's already dropped. As they turned to make a marking run, they were instructed to wait: then came the OK, and a second run was made across the target. On completing this run, there was a huge mid-air explosion behind them: apparently an aircraft had blown up and, thinking that fighters were possibly around, Woolams went into the astrodome as an extra look-out.

One navigator recorded flying 843 miles in four hours and sixteen minutes at a height of 18,000 feet. The temperature was a minimum of minus 23 degrees Celsius and the wind speed 82mph. The target was a factory on the bank of the River Elbe, which they bombed at 01.40hrs. With the windspeed on the return journey reaching 90mph, the fuel situation was becoming critical, and it was, therefore, essential that they fly a straight course back to Scampton: they reduced height to 10,000 feet where the windspeed dropped to 45mph and the temperature rose to minus eight degrees Celsius, but still had 460 miles to go before reaching their base at Scampton. When they landed at 07.36hrs, the tanks were almost empty.

Mrs Riedl, an Englishwoman married to a German, had reached Dresden as a refugee from Poland. She had just gone to bed when the sirens began to wail, and she and others made for the cellars. When they returned to the street some hours later, they found themselves in an area of burning sparks. There was no water, as the mains had been severed. As they began to clear up, the sirens went again - and the smoke from the fires began to choke them. Mrs Riedl dipped a blanket in a tub of water and put it over her head and shoulders, crouching in the middle of the road for seven hours until rain began to damp the fires down.

Squadron Leader Jordan was a prisoner in Stammlager IVB at Müchlburg-am-Elbe, midway between Leipzig and Dresden. From the camp, he was able to see the raids on Berlin, Leipzig and Dresden. The guards were not surprised that Dresden had been attacked, only that it had not been raided weeks before: they told Jordan that the city was the major communications centre for the Eastern Front and the major casualties were believed to be military personnel on their way to the Front. Considerable damage was done by the bombing to ordnance trains and dumps, which helped to create the inferno.

Tom Nelson had been shot down on a raid to Berlin in September 1943, and most of his time as a prisoner had been spent at Stalag IVB. It was a camp of about a thousand RAF P.O.W's plus many other nationalities. The camp guards were from the *Wehrmacht*. The lights went out when the air raid sirens were sounded and aircraft flew overhead. The day after the raid only half the normal number of guards were on duty as many of them lived in Dresden, about 20 miles away, and had been given special leave. When they returned, many were still very shaken and appeared to have aged by about ten years: most of them had lost someone in their family. If morale before the raid had been low, it was now completely shattered - certainly as far as the guards were concerned.

On the 13th, John Matthews was a prisoner, billeted in a hall about 25 miles from Dresden. He had been shot down over the Ruhr in 1942 on the last trip of his tour when three of his crew had been killed. The area, as far as movements on the road were concerned, was chaos. A group of girls from Hungary was being force-marched into the slaughter camps: they knew the fate awaiting them, which made it an even sadder sight. Matthews was able to talk to one of them, as she spoke English, but a few shots in the air from the guards brought the conversation to an abrupt end. The girls were mostly blue-eyed and aged about sixteen.

Another airman who was a prisoner at the time of the raid was Harold E. Cook of the USAAF. He had been shot down in May 1944. In January 1945, he was evacuated from Stalag-Luft III because the Russian troops were advancing. They marched for several days before being put on a German freight train, with sixty men in each car where there should have been forty.

The night before the raid, the train was shunted into marshalling yards at Dresden where, for twelve hours, German troops and equipment were rolled in and out. Cook described Dresden as an armed camp, with thousands of German troops, tanks and artillery, and mile upon mile of freight cars transporting the soldiers and their supplies to the East to meet the Russian advance.

Mr Nobes met another problem over France en route to Dresden: static electricity, which lit up the propellers, guns and windscreen. After two hours his eyes were running with water from watching its dagger-like effects on the windscreen, and he asked for a 'wakey-wakey' pill to maintain his concentration on the job in hand - flying a heavily loaded bomber and seven men over 800 miles. He was able to slip the pill past his oxygen mask, hoping to swallow it whole but he bit it instead and found it very bitter: spitting it all over the cockpit soon woke him up!

One aircraft of 166 Squadron had anything but an easy trip to Dresden and back. Lancaster LM 289 - Y flown by Squadron Leader Harold Whowell took off at 21.25 from its base at Kirmington, Lincolnshire. When they were 450 miles short of Dresden the starboard outer engine failed and the propeller had to be feathered. There was no hesitation and the crew decided to carry on: due to the excellent judgement of the flight engineer, Sgt Leeming, they reached Dresden on time although flying 3,000 feet below the ordered height. The target was successfully attacked and they arrived safely back at base at 08.00hrs on February 14th after a trip of ten and half hours, eight of which had been flown on three engines. Once again it had been the fine judgement of the flight engineer in conserving fuel which had enabled them to make it back home.

On 14th February 1945, Whomwell was recommended by his Commanding Officer for the immediate award of the Distinguished Flying Cross, which was granted on the 23rd.

At the time of the attack on Dresden Whomwell had flown 14 operations and was 'C' Flight Commander. At the end of their tour, Whomwell was awarded a second DFC, whilst the navigator, Pilot Officer Doll, from Canada, and the mid upper gunner, Flight Lieutenant Winstanley, received Distinguished Flying Crosses. For the excellent work of Sgt Leeming there was no reward, as was the case with many other flight engineers.

Civil defence in Dresden was directed by an engineer, but he had to contend with a series of fires over a large area, while the city's people, if they had any sense, stayed in the cellars.

The *Luftwaffe* had broadcst on the radio a series of frantic special warnings, indicating that the main targets were in the area in front of Koniev's forces heading for Dresden. The first warning said: 'Special danger for the whole Saxony industrial area'; then: 'Five waves of heavy bombers are approaching'; whilst yet another announced: 'The centre of heavy bomber activity is Chemnitz.'

Goebbels was outraged by the Allied bombing of Dresden, and proposed to Hitler that he renounce the Geneva Convention and shoot any captured enemy aircrew. Hitler at first approved this, but when a horrified aide made the Foreign Press aware of the fact, the BBC broadcast a sharp warning of retaliatory measures and the plan was soon dropped.

RAF PRU photograph taken on 14th February after three raids. (Imperial War Museum)

Dresden, February 1945, a scene of unbelievable devastation. (Imperial War Museum)

On the morning of the 14th, 1,377 aircraft were sent out by the United States Army Air Force, consisting of 1,102 B17's and 375 B24's, with a fighter escort of 857 aircraft. Of this force, 461 (of which 311 successfully attacked Dresden) were from the 1st Air Division. They attacked the city between 12.16hrs and 13.32hrs, escorted by 316 P51 fighters, of which three were shot down in combat. The town of Chemnitz was attacked at the same time by 457 aircraft of the 3rd Air Division, all of which were B17's.

The 2nd Air Division sent a force of 375 B24's to attack Magdeburg: 340 were successful. The US had first attacked Dresden on 7th October 1944, and again on 16th January 1945: later, in March and April 1945, they were to make further attacks.

The German Press was full of anger against the bomber crews. *'Terrorflieger'*, *'Luftgangster'* and *'Kindesmörders'* were just some of the headlines in the papers the next day. The Germans invented a new word to describe the damage to Dresden: 'atomisation', which meant the whole city had been blown to smithereens. This was the third term employed by the Germans to describe a great raid: the first was 'Coventrating', referring to the destruction of Coventry in 1943; then, in 1944, 'Hamburging.'

Flight Lieutenant Tom Noon, from Australia, was serving as a pilot with 97 (Pathfinder) Squadron, and was in the flare force illuminating the target in the second attack. The raid, as far as he was concerned, was just another successful operation, and there was no talk of any adverse publicity at the time. He remembers that, about a month before the Dresden raid, his squadron was briefed on three consecutive nights for a raid on Breslau, about a hundred miles east of Dresden. The intention was to fly there in cloud, and at a very low height in an attempt to stay below the German radar system. The raid was eventually cancelled because of persistent 10/10 cloud - much, he admits now, to the delight of all who were to carry out the operation.

Dresden four years later. Very little has been done other than the clearing of the streets. (Imperial War Museum)

On the 14th, a message was sent by Himmler to Alrensleben, Head of the SS in Dresden: 'I have received your report. The attacks were obviously severe, yet the very first air raid always gives the impression that the town has been completely destroyed. Take all necessary measures at once.'

CHAPTER TWELVE

DEBRIEFING

After a six-hour flight, Flight Lieutenant Topper climbed down from his aircraft: he was pleased that everything had gone according to plan and expressed his gratitude to his navigator, on whom, of course, he relied so much. In the debriefing room at Woodhall Spa, he was met by the AOC 5 Group, his Commanding Officer and various heads of departments, all wanting to know how the operation had gone.

The following morning, he received a copy of the photograph he had taken over Dresden, and was delighted by its clarity and by the confirmation it conveyed that his marking had been on target. He then went over to the teleprinter to get the first results of the raid. News of the attack came through on the BBC 6 pm bulletin. It was described as one of the more powerful blows promised by the Allied leaders at Yalta:

> 'Our pilots report that, as there was little flak, they were able to make careful and straight runs over the targets without bothering much about the defences; a terrific concentration of fires was started in the centre of the city.'

In Germany, the first published report was on 15th February in a German High Command communiqué which simply reported:

> '14th February 1945. Last night the British directed their terror-raids at Dresden.'

The night raid report No 837 stated that 85% of

Dresden had been devastated in the three-hour attack. Rail facilities and industries had suffered immense damage. The old town was reported to have been wiped out, together with most of the inner suburbs, although the outer suburbs escaped comparatively lightly. Many industries were affected, the gasworks and two tramway depots were severely damaged and railway facilities suffered most heavily. Bridges over the Elbe and public buildings were badly hit. Barracks and military establishments were less troubled, being mostly situated on the outskirts; a number of industries escaped for the same reason. But the total damage was very great indeed. The prisoners in Colditz Castle saw the attack on Dresden, which lay about thirty miles to the north-east. The Security Officer at the Castle, Reinhold Eggers, gave some idea of its impact upon the German population:

> 'People in the streets were quite demoralised by the massive attacks, even to the point of openly mocking officers in the streets for still wearing the uniform of Hitler's army.'

For the prisoners, some of whom had been 'in the bag' for five years, the attack on Dresden was the final sign of victory in the war.

The 10pm express train from Dresden *Hauptbahnhof* (main station) had been stopped as it began to leave the station: someone had apparently pulled the communication cord. Gisela Alexandra Moeltgen was on board with her husband when the announcement came that everyone had to leave the train: the police wanted them to take cover in an already overcrowded air raid shelter at the station, but their only wish was to leave the station. Their decision was correct, as 3,000 people died there, of whom 300 were still aboard the train. The Moeltgens ran to a nearby school where there was a cellar, which they hoped would provide safety from the bombers above.

Clyde Smith, an American prisoner-of-war captured in Normandy, was being forced to work, with other POWs in Dresden, digging holes for pipes in the streets. The prisoners were kept in a requisitioned school, but when the bombing started the guards opened the doors of the school and told the prisoners to get out in the street: this they did, and sought cover in the holes they had dug for the pipes.

Another American prisoner in Dresden was Henry J. Leclair, who was living in the slaughterhouse,[1] only a mile or so from the marked aiming-point. Somehow he survived all the bombing as the Germans had led him, with others, into the nearby meat-locker which was about 40 to 50 feet underground.

Jack Myers, another POW, was in a cattle truck which shunted to a stop in the marshalling yards: someone said it was Dresden. He had seen the London bombing years before and vividly remembered the noise, the smoke, the wounded, the dead and the fires. A bomb blew the locked cattle truck over, and he was able to get out into the open. He believes this saved his life, as he was convinced the prisoners would not have been fed if left in the truck.

Margaret Freyer blamed Hitler and his consorts for the raid, and not the RAF. She had been interrogated by the Gestapo in Dresden in 1943 for telling political jokes, and had been told that any recurrence of the offence would result in her being sent to a concentration camp, since her name was included on a blacklist. Now, with 41 other

[1] - *Also held prisoner in Slachthaus Fünf (Slaughterhouse five) was American Kurt Vonnengut. His experiences at Dresden were later to cause him to write his novel 'Slaughterhouse Five'.*

women, she took shelter in a cellar. When the bombing was over and she emerged into the street, she found that every second house was on fire.

The Berlin newspapers reported the attack on Dresden with such slogans as *'Terrorflieger'*, *'Luftangster'*, *'Kindermörder'*(sic), but this was not the attitude of the prisoner-of-war camp guards, some of whom had lost members of their family in the bombing at Dresden. They were in a dazed and shocked state, and incapable of feeling anything but a great sense of loss. One guard, given leave to go to Dresden, returned with the news that he could not even find the street he had lived in, let alone his house.

Heinrich Pieper heard the announcer on the wireless say that a heavy force of bombers was heading for Leipzig, but he felt that they were in fact heading for Dresden.

It was said that, in Dresden, the temperature of the fires in the centre of the Altstadt reached 3,000 degrees. On 16th February, the Berlin Correspondent of 'Expressen Stockholm' said:

> 'Berlin Government circles are greatly upset by the Allies' most concentrated attack in this war, that is, the attack on Dresden. All communications with Dresden have been cut, as the main telegraph office, the post office, the railway stations and the general headquarters were destroyed. The number of fatal casualties was disproportionately higher than in the attack on Hamburg in July 1943, because the town was more crowded with refugees from Czechoslovakia and Silesia than Berlin, and all the barracks were crammed with troops. The number of dead was reported to be 70,000.'

On the 17th, 'Svenska Morgenbladet' reported that Dresden had been completely destroyed, and that the order for its total evacuation had been given. Fatal casualties were reported to be 100.000. A refugee, who travelled by military car to Juterborg, reported that the old part of Dresden was completely destroyed, and that it was easier to count the houses still habitable in the newer parts.

The Chief of Civil Defence *Luftgaukommando III*, in a preliminary report, stated that bombs had dropped on Dresden from 22.09hrs until 22.35hrs. In the whole city area, heavy H.E. bombs had fallen, causing great fires, especially in the Inner City quarter. Hits were made on the Opera House, Catholic Hofkirche, Japanese Palace, Museum of Hygiene, Railway Directorate offices, several hospitals and the Exhibition Palace. At least 3,000 H.E. and 25,000 incendiary bombs were estimated to have been dropped. An even stronger attack was made from 01.24hrs until 01.48hrs, chiefly with H.E. bombs, some of the heaviest calibre.

A report to the Chief of *Luftgaukommando III*, Berlin-D, said that all signals communications and most police stations were out of action, and that stationary *Wehrmacht* trains with ammunition had been hit between goods stations Dresden-Neeln and Pieschen.

A report made by the *Burgomeister/Gauleiter* ARP Departments of various German cities to their Chief, *Generalmajor* W Linder, who was responsible for German Civil Defence counter measures, confirmed that the fire-storm conflagrations had caused many deaths by scorching, carbon monoxide poisoning, or suffocation in the air-raid shelters.

In Hamburg, many thousands had died, and now also in Dresden, but the firestorm raids, as they were called, were not planned as such. In order for the phenomenon of the firestorm to occur, several factors have to come together, and these cannot be predicted with great accuracy. Crucial is the adiabatic lapse rate, which is instrumental in causing core temperatures to rise at the seat of the fire and for the tremendous rate of rise of the hot gases to high altitude (as with the classic atom bomb cloud, soon to be seen for the first time). This, in turn, results in air and, in documented cases, people, being sucked towards the seat of the fire by the resulting hurricane-strength winds feeding oxygen to the fire.

The ARP officers in Dresden reported 6,000 H.E., 40,000 incendiary, 2,000 oil and 4,500 jet incendiary bombs being dropped, together with a large number of leaflets and ration cards. The Central Station was gutted and severe damage done to tracks. The Infantry Barracks and several reserve hospitals were badly damaged and gas, water and electricity services put out of action. The following industrial concerns were destroyed:

Clemens Mueller, making special instruments such as optical equipment; Glaeser Coach builders; Laube Machine works; Zeiss-Ikon; Ika, making optical and special signals equipment; Ernemann, making fuses and optical instruments; Universal, making weapon parts and torpedoes; Seidetz, making small arms; Lohman, making anti-aircraft and field guns; Saxoniawerke, making gears and differentials; Chemische Fabrik Geye A.G, producing poison gas; AG für Cartounagen-industrie, supplying paper for munitions and shell linings; an oil refinery producing special oil for aviation, also used as a mixture for all lubricating oils; Sachsenwerk, making submarine engines. All were gutted or severely damaged.

In Stockholm, propaganda was published in the newspaper '*Das Reich*' with a long article on the 'The Dresden Catastrophe.' The city was represented as a purely cultural centre, with no mention of its great war factories or its importance as a transport centre behind the

Eastern Front, and the reason behind the propaganda became clearer. The theme of the article was that Dresden could only be spoken of in the past tense: it was all part of the big back-down before the *Reich* collapsed. A German appeal to the world was being made before the guns stopped firing, and it went along these lines:

1. Destruction of German culture by bombing and the continuation of the war would be an irreparable loss to the world.

2. Such political differences existed inside Germany that practically no Germans could ever have been real Nazis.
3. Unless the Allies made a quick and easy peace possible for Germany, Bolshevism would rule the world.

The fire station headquarters was hit, and firemen dropped dead from their vehicles as they drove through the burning streets. They were ordered, at all costs, to save the three principal railway stations in order to maintain supplies to the troops fighting only 50 miles further east.

It was announced in Germany that corpses were a problem, and that flame throwers were being used to burn hundreds of bodies huddled in craters and cellars. Numerous funeral pyres, each built of railway sleepers and topped with 400 to 500 of the bodies which had been found in the streets, were set alight along the centres of the ruined boulevards and roadways. Special units, many using Allied POWs, were dispatched through the ruined city armed with hatchets and buckets, their task being to hack the ring-fingers from the thousands of dead and remove their wedding rings before the bodies were heaped on the pyres for burning. It was tradition for married couples to have their names inscribed on the inside of the rings and, thus, some casualties could be identified and officially recorded.

A well-informed senior *Luftwaffe* officer stated, at the end of the war:

> 'Pressure by the Gestapo succeeded for a long time in maintaining artificial morale, in spite of intense bombardment, but that a limit to this could be reached was clearly exemplified in the case of Dresden. When this catastrophe became known to the whole of Germany, morale disintegrated everywhere, in spite of the best or worst efforts of the Gestapo.'

At the debriefing John Woolams attended, no one had much desire for conversation: even the ground-crew were unusually quiet. The bomb aimer, when asked if he thought the bombing had been accurate, nodded once but did not speak.

Jack Holden, having been obliged to fly at a reduced speed to save fuel, heard the BBC News while still airborne. He and his crew were due for seven days leave, commencing that morning. After a hasty wash and breakfast, they all went their separate ways. Holden arrived home a few hours later, somewhat tired and crumpled, and was met by his mother with the remark: 'What dirty boots you have.' He went to the cinema during his leave. The newsreel showed the bombing of Dresden, and he felt considerably impressed.

Bob Ryett had no sooner got to bed when he was called out again before lunch to prepare for a raid on Chemnitz.

Deryck Thurman was also on the Chemnitz raid: he got to bed about 9am and was woken at 3pm, for another long trip of eight and a half hours.

Reg Small remembers great excitement as they all

came to the conclusion that they had done a good job on Dresden, and were very pleased with themselves.

Joe Williams' aircraft landed at Kelstern in daylight at 07.07hrs, after a flight of nine and a half hours. After debriefing and breakfast, he had just got to bed, at 11am, when the Tannoy blared out: 'All crews report for run-ups.' There was another op. to Chemnitz that night, but it proved less successful than Dresden because of the weather.

Ken Hamilton, a pilot with 195 Squadron, got to bed at 10am and was woken for another long trip to Chemnitz, involving eighteen hours flying, after only four and half hours sleep.

Richard Thomas, also a pilot, remembers the debriefing and the crew complaining about the near-misses involving other aircraft, in response to which one debriefing officer asked: 'Did you get their squadron lettering?' Another suggested that they should have used their Aldis lamp to read the lettering, and a third suggested that they might have switched on their navigation lights. In theory, the main force was supposed to fly at a height of 16,000 feet for heavy bombers and 19,000 feet for Mosquitos, whilst 'Race Course Pattern' aircraft flew at 17,500 feet, but to reach that level they had to endure turbulence from the slipstream of the other aircraft which had just passed. Between January and April 1945, an average of eighteen aircraft each month were lost due to collision.

The first-full length bulletin was released by the Air Ministry on the morning of 14th February 1945. It stressed the importance of Dresden as a railway network, and the fact that the buildings in Dresden had been used for housing troops and administrative offices which had moved there from other bombed-out cities and towns in Germany. It went on to outline the factories in Dresden, and what they were manufacturing for the war effort. The Germans responded by saying that all they were making was toothpaste and baby-powder.

On 16th February, at the Supreme HQ of the Allied Expeditionary Forces under General Eisenhower in Paris, at an 'off the record' Press conference, Air Commodore Colin Grierson, the Assistant Chief of Staff A-2, responsible for the conduct of all air operations (including information about targets for attack) described how the air forces planned to bomb large population centres, and afterwards prevent supplies from getting through. In the course of this conference, in response to a question, the Air Commodore referred to German allegations of 'terror raids'. This stuck in the mind of the correspondent from the Associated Press and, within an hour, his report was despatched on Paris radio and cabled to America for inclusion in the morning papers:

> 'Allied air chiefs have made the long-awaited decision to adopt deliberate terror-bombing of German population centres as a ruthless expedient of hastening Hitler's doom. More raids, such as those recently carried out by heavy bombers of the Allied air forces on residential sections of Berlin, Dresden, Chemnitz and Kottbus, are in store for the Germans, for the avowed purpose of heaping more confusion on Nazi road and rail traffic, and to sap German morale. The all-out air war on Germany became obvious with the unprecedented daylight assault on the refugee-crowded capital, with civilians fleeing from the Red tide in the East.'

A summary of Grierson's statement was written by General Carl Spaatz's Deputy Commander of Operations, Major F.L Anderson:

> 'The effect of the heavy raids on population centres has always been, first of all, to cause the Germans to bring in train-loads of supplies of extra comforts, and take away the population which had been rendered homeless. Now, that form of relief relies to a pretty great extent on paid and sound (sic) communications between the big cities and the whole of the interior of Germany itself, so that the destruction of not only communications centres, but also of the towns where the relief comes from and where the evacuees go to, are very definitely operations which contribute greatly towards the break-up of the German economic system.'

He added that Grierson had said that the attacks on Dresden and other targets near the Russian front were as a result of recommendations made by the combined strategic targets committee. He had stated that the reasons for such attacks were:

(1) They were the centres to which evacuees were being moved.

(2) They were the centres of communications through which traffic was moving across the Russian Front, and from the Western Front to the East.

(3) They were sufficiently close to the Russian Front for the Russians to continue the successful prosecution of their battle.

Anderson's report showed that Grierson had concluded his statement by saying that the principal aim of attacks such as that on Dresden would be to stop communications carrying military supplies, rather than to create confusion among refugees.

The British Government, which received news of the SHAEF Press conference at 7.30pm on the evening of 17th February, imposed a ban on the publication of the despatch. On the 18th, correspondent Howard Cowan wrote in 'The Washington Star' that the Allied commanders had made the long-awaited decision to adopt deliberate terror-bombing of the great German population centres as a ruthless expedient to hasten Hitler's doom.

This caused an uproar in the American High Command. General Arnold spoke to General Spaatz on the 18th, demanding an explanation as to the directives and priorities for strategic bombing. On the 19th came the reply, in which Spaatz said that the article was an exaggeration of what had been said by Air Commodore Grierson, which had slipped past the censors, and that there was no change in the basic policy, in that all targets were deemed to be of military importance.

At 10.30pm on the 18th, 'Lord Haw-Haw', William Joyce, came on the air from Germany with his well-known and hated announcement, 'Germany Calling', about the bombing of Dresden:

> 'British propagandists are boasting that, by attacking such cities as Dresden, the RAF and US air force are co-operating with the Soviets. They do not remember any occasion on which the Soviet High Command has troubled itself to co-operate with British efforts. Incidentally, Eisenhower's Headquarters have now issued a stupid and impudent denial of the obvious truth that the bombing of German towns has a terrorist motive. Churchill's spokesmen, both in the Press and on the radio, have actually gloried in the air attacks on Berlin and Dresden, and on the refugees from the East. Various British

> journalists have written as if the murdering of German refugees were a first-class military achievement. I shall always remember how, alluding to the attack on Dresden, one BBC announcer happily prattled: "There is no china in Dresden today." That was, perhaps, meant to be a joke; but in what sort of taste? Far be it from me to strike a sentimental note amidst the grim and dark realities of this phase in a gigantic struggle, which is destined to decide more than the fate of porcelain'.

He concluded by talking about the architectural treasures destroyed in Dresden, and the fate of the refugees. It was announced, in radio transmissions to the USA, that the *Wehrmacht* had awarded General Spaatz the Order of the White Feather for his part in the crime of attacking Dresden.

On 6th March 1945, the Member of Parliament for Ipswich, Mr R R Stokes, accused the Government of war crimes in a debate in the House of Commons, with the support of the Marquess of Salisbury and the Bishop of Chichester, Doctor Bell, who had, since 1942, been opposed to the bombing policy. An official denial was made, a month later, that Bomber Command was not involved in purely terror tactics or the killing of German women and children.

In Germany, at the same time, Dr Joseph Goebbels recorded in his diary that he had been visited by Ludolf von Alvensleben, Dresden's SS police chief. He had told him of the Dresden catastrophe, and that nothing like it had been seen before.

On 6th March 1945, the bombing of Dresden was reviewed by the Secretary of State for War in the USA. He was informed by General George C Marshall, the Chief of Staff, that Dresden had been bombed because it was a communications centre of great importance, through which reinforcements passed to reach the Russian Front; and because the city was clearly related to German potential for launching a counter-attack against the southern wing of the Russian offensive; and that standard bombing methods had been used in the Allied air attacks against Dresden.

With this statement to the Secretary, the issue of the Dresden bombings within the framework of established bombing policies was considered closed. It was considered that, if the attacks on the communications centres to the Eastern Front had not been successful, the European war would have been prolonged. At the time Dresden was attacked, Marshal Koniov's armies were less than 70 miles east of Dresden and, by virtue of their extended positions, highly vulnerable to German counter-attack, provided the Germans could pass reinforcements through Dresden. With communications through Dresden made impossible as a consequence of the Allied bombing, the Russian salient in that area remained safe throughout the ensuing months of the war.

On 23rd March, a message was sent to Stalin by Eisenhower, outlining plans for the total defeat of German ground forces to the West and stating that his final task would be to divide the enemy's forces by 'joining hands' with the Russians. He went on to say that the best axis to effect the junction of forces was a line through Erfurt-Leipzig-Dresden. Stalin replied on 1st April 1945, saying that the plan outlined by Eisenhower was in line with the views of the Soviet High Command: he also agreed on the proposed axis.

On 27th April 1945, American and Russian forces joined up near Leipzig, and Hitler's army had been cut in two. On 8th May, the Russians entered and captured Dresden, and the war in Europe was over.

By February 1945, Hitler's army had been almost

exhausted. The Ruhr lay in ruins, and most of Upper Silesia was in Russian hands. Production of coal and steel had been reduced to one-fifth of the volume of the summer of 1944 and, owing to the dislocation of rail and water transport, only a fraction of Ruhr output could be moved to the factories of Central and Southern Germany. Production of arms and munitions was about half the rate of 1944.

Hitler was still convinced that the new jet aircraft would influence the outcome of the war but, by February 1945, only 283 Me 262 fighters had been built, and the airfields they needed were soon spotted from the air and bombed. He had been trying to neutralise the port of Antwerp to delay the Allied offensive but, with an output of only 1,500 V1 and V2 missiles a month, the number required to saturate the area was not available.

On 19th March 1945, Hitler issued an order to all *Gauleiters*, with no regard at all for his own people, that everything which could be of immediate use to the enemy was to be destroyed; i.e all industrial plants, electrical facilities, water and gas works and all food and clothing stores. He also ordered the destruction of all forms of transport which might aid the mobility of the enemy. It was only by the intervention of Dr Albert Speer that this order was not carried out to the full.

The overall plan by Eisenhower after the D-Day landings was for the primary and secondary efforts to link up in the Kassel area, and then thrust forward to the East: this thrust would be directed at the Leipzig-Dresden region because it contained the greater part of remaining German industrial capacity, and was the zone to which the German Ministries were believed to be moving.

On 28th March 1945, Winston Churchill, the man who had ordered the bombing of Dresden, sent a personal telegram to General Ismay, his Chief of Staff (see over),

TOP SECRET DCAS

PRIME MINISTER'S
PERSONAL TELEGRAM
SERIAL No. D.83/5.

GENERAL ISMAY FOR C.O.S. COMMITTEE.
C.A.S.

It seems to me that the moment has come when the question of bombing of German cities simply for the sake of increasing the terror, though under other pretexts, should be reviewed. Otherwise we shall come into control of an utterly ruined land. We shall not, for instance, be able to get housing materials out of Germany for our own needs because some temporary provision would have to be made for the Germans themselves. The destruction of Dresden remains a serious query against the conduct of Allied bombing. I am of the opinion that military objectives must henceforward be more strictly studied in our own interests rather than that of the enemy.

The Foreign Secretary has spoken to me on this subject, and I feel the need for more precise concentration upon military objectives, such as oil and communications behind the immediate battle-zone, rather than on mere acts of terror and wanton destruction, however impressive.

(Intld.) W.S.C.

28.3.45.

indicating that he had had second thoughts about the bombing of cities and, in particular, the Saxon capital Dresden. Only two months earlier he had been the advocator of this campaign. The signal exasperated his Chief of Air Staff, Portal, who immediately asked his deputy, Air Vice Marshal Norman Bottomley, to obtain Harris's comments, although apparently Harris never saw the actual signal.

Bottomley's letter to Harris, which he requested should be treated as personal, read as follows:

'Dear C-in-C,

At the instigation of the Prime Minister, we have just been asked to consider whether the time has come when the question of bombing of German cities "simply for the sake of increasing the terror, though under other pretexts" should not be reviewed. One of the reasons given is that we shall not, for instance, be able to get housing material out of Germany for our own needs because some temporary provision would ultimately have to be made for the Germans themselves. The note comments on the destruction of Dresden as a serious query against the conduct of Allied bombing, and expresses the opinion that military objectives must henceforward be more strictly studied in our own interests rather than those of the enemy. Finally, the note states that there is need for more precise concentration upon military objectives, such as oil and communications behind the immediate battle-zone, rather than on mere acts of terror and wanton destruction, however impressive. I am sure you will agree that this note mis-interprets the purpose of our attacks on industrial areas in the past, and appears to ignore the aim given by the combined Chiefs of Staff in their directives, which have been blessed by the heads of Governments. As you know, the overall mission of the Strategic Air Forces in Europe has been given as "the progressive destruction and dislocation of the German military industrial and economic system, and the direct support of land and naval forces." Our attacks on industrial areas have been ordered with this aim in view. There has never been any instruction issued which gives any foundation to an allegation that German cities have been attacked simply for the sake of increasing terror. From time to time in the past you have commented on the tremendous contribution which the destruction of German industrial areas has made towards the crippling of the enemy's war economy. There may now be sound political reasons for abandoning our attacks on German cities, but these reasons should be balanced against the contribution which we are making thereby in crippling German war economy and in hastening the military defeat of the enemy. The CAS feels that, before we submit an official reply to the note, you should be given an opportunity of commenting on the opinions described above. He would be glad to have your comments, both on the allegations which are made as to our efforts in the past, and as to the wisdom of the proposal for discontinuing these attacks and, instead, confining ourselves to what is described as "more precise concentration upon military objectives such as oil and communications behind the immediate battle-zone." Since this object will be considered early next week by the COS, and probably the Defence Committee, the CAS would be glad if we could have your views as early as possible.'

Even before he replied, Portal had persuaded Churchill to withdraw his original signal concerning bombing policy, and to redraft it in such a way as to deal only with the point of area bombing. The particular passage which he felt should be changed was: '...the bombing of German cities has been for the sake of increasing the terror, though under other pretexts.'

D.C.A.S.

The Prime Minister agreed this evening to withdraw his recent minute about bombing policy, and to redraft it in such a way as to deal only with the question whether it is in our own interests at this stage of the war to continue with area bombing.

2. You need, therefore, deal only with this point in your draft reply, and it will be unnecessary to deal comprehensively with the value of area bombing in the destruction of industry in the past.

28th March, 1945. C.A.S.

Portal then issued the following instruction:

'The reply should make it clear that our action against German cities has not been for the purpose of inspiring terror, but has been strictly in accordance with the directive given by the combined Chiefs of Staff and blessed by the Heads of the two Governments. The overall mission of the Strategic Air Forces, according to this directive, has been "the progressive destruction and dislocation of the German military industrial and economic system, and the direct support of the land and naval forces".'

The new draft was to be ready no later than mid-day on Monday, 2nd April. On 29th March, Bottomley sent a memo to Portal:

> 'You will recollect that you did not wish the Prime Minister's minute on the subject of bombing of cities to be sent out to C-in-C Bomber Command, since you regarded this as a personal minute to yourself. I accordingly sent out the attached letter and have received a reply dated 29th March from the C-in-C. I thought you would like to see this at once.'

On the same day Harris replied:

'Dear Norman,

It is difficult to answer indictments of which the terms are not fully revealed, and for this reason I cannot deal as thoroughly as I would like to with the points raised in your letter of the 28th. I take it, however, that it is unnecessary for me to make any comment on the passages which you quote and which, without the context, are abusive in effect, though doubtless not in intention. To suggest that we have bombed German cities "simply for the sake of increasing the terror though under other pretexts" and to speak of our offensive as including "mere acts of terror and wanton destruction" is an insult both to the bombing policy of the Air Ministry and to the manner in which that policy has been executed by Bomber Command. This sort of thing, if it deserves an answer, will certainly receive none from me, after three years of implementing official policy.

As regards the specific points raised in your letter, namely the adverse economic effects on ourselves by increasing yet further the material havoc in Germany and the destruction of Dresden* in particular, the answer is surely very simple. It is already demonstrated in the liberated countries that what really makes any sort of recovery almost impossible is less the destruction of buildings than the complete dislocation of transportation. If, therefore, this objection is to be taken seriously, I suggest that the transportation plan, rather than the strategic bombing of cities, is what needs to be reconsidered, as I understand it has been, and for precisely that reason. You will remember that Dresden was recommended by the Targets Committee as a transportation target, as well as on other grounds.

I do not, however, stress this point since I assume that what is really at issue is (a) whether our strategic bombing policy up to date has been justified, and (b) whether the time has now come to discontinue this policy. I will therefore confine myself to these questions.

As regards (a) I have on previous occasions discussed this matter very fully in official correspondence with the Air Ministry. I have always held, and still maintain, that my Directive, which you quote, "the progressive destruction and dislocation of the German military, industrial and economic systems" could be carried out only by the elimination of German industrial cities, and not merely by attacks on individual factories, however important these might be in themselves. This view was also officially confirmed by the Air Ministry. The overwhelming evidence which is now available to support it makes it quite superfluous for me to argue at length that the destruction of those cities has weakened the German war effort and is now enabling Allied soldiers to advance into the heart of Germany with negligible casualties. Hence, the only question which I have to answer is this: would "confining ourselves to more precise concentration upon military objectives such as oil and communications behind the immediate battle zone" tend to shorten the war more than persistence in attacks on cities? The answer appears to me to be obvious; but, even if it is not, I must point out, as I have frequently done before, that we have by no means always a free choice in this matter. Weather conditions frequently constrain me to decide between attacking cities and not attacking at all. When this happens, it is surely evident that it is expedient to attack the cities. I can only find, pinpoint and hit small isolated targets with a small part of my force at a time, and I have not enough fighter escort to do more than two small attacks daily.

I have thus disposed of point (a). We have never gone in for terror bombing and the attacks which we have made in accordance with my Directive have in fact produced the strategic consequences for which they were designed and from which the Armies now profit. Point (b) is rather difficult to follow. It can hardly mean that attacks on cities no longer produce dislocation in the German war effort. Quite the contrary is the case. The nearer Germany is to collapse, the less capable she is of re-organising to meet disasters of this kind, and we ought logically to make a special effort to eliminate the few cities which still remain more or less serviceable.

I therefore assume that the view under consideration is something like this: "No doubt in the past we were justified in attacking German cities. But to do so was always repugnant and, now that the Germans are beaten anyway, we can properly abstain from proceeding with these attacks." This is a doctrine to which I could never subscribe. Attacks on cities, like any other act of war, are intolerable unless they are strategically justified. But they are strategically justified in so far as they tend to shorten the war and so preserve the lives of Allied soldiers. To my mind we have absolutely no right to give them up unless it is certain that they will not have this effect. I do not personally regard the whole of the remaining war cities of Germany as worth the bones of one British Grenadier. It therefore seems to me that there is one, and only one, valid argument on which a case for giving up strategic bombing could be based; namely for the Armies to do nothing except to occupy Germany against unorganised resistance. If this is what is meant, I shall no doubt be informed of it. It does not, however, appear to be the view of the Supreme Commander. Until it is, I submit that the strategic bombing of German cities must go on.

Some final points. As you know, transportation targets are now largely off. Oil has had, and is getting, all we can practically give it in consideration of weather and escort factors. We answer every army support call and, as Monty tells us, in a "decisive manner." We have asked for more, but there aren't any. H.E. is seriously limited in supply. Incendiaries are not. All these factors must therefore also be considered, and the inevitable answer is that either we continue as in the past, or we very largely stand down altogether. The last alternative would certainly be welcome. I take little delight in the work, and none whatever in risking my crews. Japan remains. Are we going to bomb their cities flat - as in Germany - and give the Armies a walkover - as in France and Germany - or are we going to bomb only their outlying factories** and subsequently invade at the cost of 3 to 6 million casualties? We should be careful of precedents.

Yours ever, Bert

* The feeling, such as there is, over Dresden could be easily explained by any psychiatrist. It is connected with German bands and Dresden shepherdesses. Actually Dresden was a mass of munitions works, an intact government centre, and a key transportation point to the east. It is now none of these things.

**Largely underground by the time we got going.

(The two notes refer to the text of the letter).

On 30th March, at the 83rd meeting of the Chiefs of Staff Committee, Churchill withdrew his minute of the 28th and on 1st April 1945 substituted the following to General Ismay:

'It seems to me that the moment has come when the question of the so called "area bombing" of German cities should be reviewed from the point of view of our own interests. If we come into control of an entirely ruined land, there will be a great shortage of accommodation for ourselves and our allies, and we shall be unable to get housing materials out of Germany for our own needs because some temporary provision would have to be made for the Germans themselves. We must see to it that our attacks do not do more harm to ourselves in the long run than they do to the enemy's immediate war effort. Pray let me have your views.'

The conclusions reached by the Chief of Staff on 6th April were as follows:

(i) Area bombing designed solely with the object of destroying or disorganising industrial areas should be discontinued.

(ii) There should be no alteration to the current bombing directive such as would exclude area bombing.

(iii) Area attacks might prove necessary against those targets the destruction of which was calculated best to assist the advance of the Allied Armies into Germany, or to have the most immediate effect upon the enemy's ability to continue armed resistance.

(iv) Any ultimate political or economic disadvantage of area bombing necessitated by these operations should be accepted.

It was requested that these proposals be accepted by the Combined Chiefs of Staff. The Air Staff also postulated that there were situations in which area bombing would be valid. For example, such attacks might be made on built-up areas behind the Fronts containing reserves and maintenance organisations, in the event of resistance stiffening on the Western or Eastern Fronts; and on communications systems in Central and Eastern Germany when the time factor might make it impossible to wait for visual conditions for precise bombing.

The revised memorandum was accepted by the Air Staff but the stigma remained. Harris himself found it very hard to accept that Churchill had written such words about the way in which Bomber Command was fighting the war, particularly after he had asked, only three months earlier, for targets such as Dresden to be attacked.

There were people in Dresden who blamed Hitler for the raids, rather than the RAF, saying that he had begun the trouble, and they were now reaping the Allies' wrath.

Some of the prisoner-of-war camp guards were still convinced that the V-weapons would win them the war, whilst others were saying that the war was over and that they could not survive.

CHAPTER THIRTEEN

DEFENCES AND LOSSES

In September 1942, Hitler had already ordered that young people, including schoolchildren, were to be called up for service on flak units. The defences at Pilsen, which was the same distance from England as Dresden, were increased but, when no further attacks were forthcoming, it was thought Dresden was in no danger because of the flying range involved.

In January 1943, Dresden had only three batteries of 88mm guns and 4 light flak batteries for firing barrages. It was felt these were too few to protect a population of 600,000 people and, in August 1943, the defences were strengthened. The additional artillery sent to Dresden consisted of captured Soviet 85mm and 88mm guns: the problems were the lack of rangefinders, and the shortage of gunners. It was assumed that bomber attacks would come from the north-west, following the line of the Elbe.

The attacks on Leipzig in 1943/44 had no effect on the defences at Dresden. But the *Battle of Berlin* attacks did have some effect, and in 1944 the defences in Dresden were again strengthened: the city was now defended by seven batteries of 50 guns, plus five batteries of 28 Russian guns. These guns were fired in September 1944, during the American attacks. However, by December the guns in Chemnitz and Dresden (including the Russian batteries) had been removed. All that remained were three heavy batteries of 24 guns, with no light flak, searchlights, or smokescreen devices. It was reported that the guns removed had been transported to the Russian Front. However, it is highly probable that, even if a fully mobile and effective defence system had been in place, the results of the attack on Dresden would have been the same.

The Intelligence reports produced by the RAF after the attack described the flak as negligible at Dresden, but moderate and gradually increasing at Bohlen. Fighter opposition was slight, the cloud cover and use of WINDOW obviously deceiving the German fighter controllers to the extent that only nine of the 1,164 bombers which returned from the raid on Dresden reported being attacked. One aircraft was lost at Bohlen, one over Dresden in the first attack, having been hit by a bomb from an aircraft above, and four in the second attack - one while approaching the Somme estuary outbound, and the other in the target area.

Several aircraft made forced landings in France, mainly because of fuel shortage, but only one of these aircraft was wrecked. Two aircraft were destroyed in landing or taxiing accidents in the UK.

The Intruder operations were very successful: 83 Mosquitos, including 24 from Fighter Command, made 21 interceptions and destroyed 2 Me 110's north of Frankfurt. It was reported that only one Me 110 took off in the area of Dresden, that being shot down by light flak from its own base defences.

A number of accounts have been written since the war about the number of people killed in Dresden in February 1945: perhaps the actual total killed will never be known. One estimate suggested 30,000 killed or missing. The German Ministry of Propaganda announced a death toll of between 350,000 and 400,000. A Swiss agency reported that 100,000 had been killed.

In 1963, it was announced in David Irving's book, *'The Destruction of Dresden'*, that 135,000 had been killed in the three attacks. It stated that there were a million people in the city that night, of whom 350,000 were refugees from the Eastern Front, which would have meant the highest city population in Germany after that of Berlin.

In 1965, new evidence indicated that the estimated death toll had been grossly exaggerated, and that the actual figure was 25,000, with 35,000 missing.

Herr Schill, the Mayor of Dresden in 1985, confirmed that 35,000 had been identified as dead, with perhaps another 10,000 unidentified. He went on to say that the Western media had tried to compare the destruction of Dresden with the bombing of Hiroshima to show that the atomic bomb was not so bad, and to minimise the effect of nuclear war. (His predecessor, Walter Weideuer, had claimed that the Americans had planned to drop the atom bomb on Dresden if it had been ready in time.) Schill went on to say that the Red Army had liberated and not conquered Germany, and that he felt gratitude towards the Russians: he also referred to the 'barbaric destruction' of the world famous city by the British and Americans.

In November 1940, German attacks on Coventry brought 380 deaths and 800 injured. In Rotterdam, earlier, 980 people were killed in an air attack and, in Hamburg, in July 1943, 42,800 people were killed in three attacks by the RAF. In the attacks on the UK, including the Blitz in 1941, 51,500 people had been killed. Such casualties are not uncommon in war. In Germany 500,000 were estimated as being killed in air attacks, whereas nearly two million military personnel lost their lives. Against this, nearly six million Jews were slaughtered by the Germans. The Russians lost over eight million military personnel and seven million civilians. The British lost nearly 400,000 military personnel and over 63,000 civilians. The losses to Bomber Command were in the order of 56,000 airmen killed and over 9,000 taken prisoner.

Ursula Kretschmer was 21 and living in Dresden at the time of the attack and, even when the warning came, did not believe it would happen until she saw what the Germans described as 'Christmas Trees' (the marker flares of red, white, and green) in the sky over the city.

It was as bright as day. The noise of aircraft engines was deafening, and she thought her ears would burst. When she was asked, many years later, if she felt bitter towards the British and Americans, she said that it was war and that many terrible things had to be done at such times. The guilty ones, she said, were those who gave the orders.

In the first wave attack one Lancaster of 463 Squadron was destroyed and, in the second, five aircraft were lost.

An aircraft of 166 Squadron, flown by Pilot Officer Churchward, had just completed its bombing run over Dresden when it was hit by a burst of heavy flak which made several holes in the fuselage and also blew one of the incendiaries back into the aircraft. It ignited, but the wireless operator managed (despite a lack of oxygen) to extinguish the fire: the navigator's log, however, was lost through one of the holes in the fuselage but, despite this, he managed to bring the aircraft back only 5 miles off track.

Lancaster D-Dog of 115 Squadron, flown by Flying Officer Dick Archibald, took off from Witchford at 21.50hrs and bombed the target at 01.30hrs. Twenty minutes later, at a height of 20,000 feet, the starboard inner engine started to lose oil pressure: eventually, the pressure dropped to zero, and the engine was feathered, but only with some difficulty. The flak en route had been very slight and bursting below them, so the cause of the problem was unknown. They continued on three engines but three hours and twenty minutes later, when diving to reduce height in accordance with briefing instructions, the feathered engine started revving at 1,200 rpm. The pilot tried the coarse pitch lever, but was unable to move it; the engine started to fire erratically and the revolutions increased to 3,800. A shower of sparks came from the engine, and the whole aircraft began to vibrate badly. Soon flames appeared underneath the engine, the area behind it began to get red hot and sparks were seen going back past the rear turret. The pilot gave the order to bale out when the aircraft was down to 4,000 feet and on a rather erratic course. All the crew baled out successfully and landed safely except the mid upper gunner, Sgt George Preston, who was killed on landing: he was found three miles from the crashed aircraft, wearing neither a parachute nor a harness. These were found near the crashed aircraft, which had dived in about four miles from where the crew had landed. The leg strap of the parachute harness was wrenched away where it attached to the back strap, and the canopy was torn. It was assumed that Preston had become caught up on the aircraft when baling out, and had fallen out of his harness when the strap gave way: one of his boots had been pulled off and the parachute had become detached, either when the aircraft had dived or when it had hit the ground and disintegrated.

To say that the *Luftwaffe* was no longer an effective force at the time of the raid on Dresden would be untrue: between 14th February and the end of the war in Europe over 300 Allied bombers were lost.

In March 1945, Dresden was again bombed by the US Air Force. On this occasion, they were attacked by jet fighters, thirty five of which led three large formations of other fighters: they were scrambled in the expectation that Berlin was again to be the target, but 75 of them were able to head for Dresden and the Ruhr area, attacking the bombers when they were nine minutes away from Dresden. Six of the leading group were shot down by the jets, which had to withdraw because of fuel shortage.

One German, a Ju 88 pilot of NJG 100, wrote in his diary:

> 'My saddest day as a night-fighter. Huge firework display over the city. Jockenhoffer shot down by our own anti-aircraft guns. Second scramble before 2am. No communications with divisional headquarters. Apparently Division was in the dark. Result: major attack on Dresden, in which the city was smashed to smithereens - and we were standing by and looking on. How can such a thing be possible? One's mind turns more and more to sabotage, or at least a certain irresponsible defeatism among the 'gentlemen' up there. Feeling that things are approaching an end with giant strides. What then? Poor Germany!'

The night after the Dresden raid, the target was Chemnitz, forty miles from the ruined city, and an industrial concern making ammunition boxes was destroyed. Losses were relatively slight, with ten aircraft failing to return.

In two days Bomber Command had flown 1,522 sorties and dropped 5,256 tons of bombs, while the American Eighth had flown 1,266 missions and dropped 3,050 tons of bombs on three cities near the Russian Front.

CHAPTER FOURTEEN

REFLECTIONS

The men who took part in the operation to Dresden are now in their sixties, seventies and, in some cases, eighties. They came from all manner of social and academic backgrounds. The method of forming a bomber crew was perhaps bizarre but, somehow, it worked very well and the great majority of crews gelled together into very efficient, dedicated and courageous teams. From this experience came a lifetime of friendship and comradeship which cannot be surpassed.

How do they feel today, 50 years later, about the attack which, over that period, has marred the reputation of the overall effort and contribution by Bomber Command in WWII? The memories and thoughts of many of the men who were on the Dresden operation are similar, in that they were all fighting for a common cause - freedom for Great Britain and the world.

After the war Bob Nelson visited Celle in Germany, a city which had escaped much of the fighting, and was rich with 'olde worlde' shops and houses. Probably, he felt, Dresden would once have been similar, and he was aware that many people regretted its destruction. To those people, Nelson recommended the short journey from Celle to Belsen to enable them to realise what Bomber Command and others had fought to eradicate: Hitler and his Nazi party had much to answer for. As a very small cog in the magnificent fighting machine that was Bomber Command, Nelson felt privileged to have helped in the fight for freedom for all those oppressed and persecuted under the Nazi regime. Sadly, in December 1994, Bob Nelson died.

Jack Holden reflects today that war can never be

entirely right: there comes a point where there is no alternative and a 'just' war has to be waged to prevent freedom and civil liberties being extinguished. The loss of life, Holden feels, is always to be regretted, and he is particularly sad about the many bomber crews who were killed. His view is that when so many soldiers and civilians are being lost it is time to settle for peace: however, Hitler was not prepared to lose face, and dragged WWII on for at least two months longer than was necessary. Holden also considers that no war should never be continued without the support of the civilian population.

Whenever Joe Nutt is criticised for taking part in the Dresden operation, he quotes from the Bible:

> 'Who art thou to judge another man's servant?
> To his own master he standeth or falleth.'

George Futer says that the damage and loss of life was horrendous, and that it was unfortunate that the city was thrust into the position of being a tactical target: that fact alone sealed its fate. But, having said that, Futer, a Canadian, makes no apologies for having attacked Dresden. Any action, he maintains, which was designed to shorten the war was its own justification. At no time during his Air Force service did George ever enjoy destruction for its own sake, and he had no qualms about the raid on Dresden other than that it involved a long 'stooge' across the breadth of Germany.

Bob Davies has memories and thoughts very near to home. The trip to Dresden at the time was just another operation. If he had thought at all of the awful suffering on the ground, it would have been with a sense of 'so what'. He did not feel sorry for Dresden, and he has neither regrets that he was there nor any feeling of guilt. His mother's parents were, as he puts it, far from ordinary.

Her mother was a Scot and her father a German. Her oldest sister married a German, and her second sister an Austrian, whilst her third married Bob's father in Malta, where he was a British naval officer. On the outbreak of war, his father rejoined the Navy, Bob the RAF, and one of his cousins the *Luftwaffe*: he became a flak gunner, and served in Jersey before going to the Russian Front.

In WWI, his father had led a flotilla of minesweepers for three years. He had had two ships mined under him, but had managed to beach them on each occasion. He was buried alive for five hours when a bomb destroyed the hotel he was staying in, and he died post-war of cancer attributed to that bombing incident.

When it became known that his cousin, serving in Jersey, had relations in the British forces, the cousin was sent to the Russian Front and lost a leg on the last day of the war. His two girl cousins, living in Czechoslovakia, were intercepted by Czech partisans as they tried to reach Germany. They, and the whole party they were with, were lined up and shot: the older girl died instantly, falling across her sister who had been shot in the head. Somehow the younger girl survived, and is still alive today in Munich, although she has continual headaches, as a result of a fragment of lead lodged near her brain, which will always remind her of the war.

During a visit to Dresden in 1993, Angus Belford met some of the survivors of the attack in circumstances which he describes as friendly. In the central square, he found a statue to a national hero on horseback, surrounded by a tiled area. Somehow it had survived the bombing, which the guide said must have been through divine intervention. In conversation with the locals, they agreed that there had been red fires in the square during the attack: Bedford felt that the square had been identified by the Pathfinders and marked as an aiming point which, ironically, had saved it from direct attack.

Kenneth Gooch was shocked, some years after the war, to learn that at least 38,000 people had been killed in the attack but, as in the cases of Hiroshima and Nagasaki, he felt the raid had been necessary to shorten the war. He reminds us all to remember Coventry, London and Poland, and the fact that, in WWI, Scarborough was bombarded by the German Navy.

Roland Ward wants everyone to remember the thousands of men who left Australia, Canada, South Africa and New Zealand to fight with Bomber Command and to help Britain in its hour of need. Far from being war criminals, they were helping to bring the war to an end, and to save lives that would have been lost if it had been prolonged.

Ramsey Turner remembers that it was the actions of Bomber Command which forced the Germans to concentrate on building fighters for defence instead of a larger bomber force to attack Britain and other targets in the world, so he has no feeling of guilt at all.

Kenneth Johnson, a former bomb aimer, says that, apart from the great destruction and loss of life, he did not have any thoughts other than those he'd had about previous operations against Germany. Having bombed the Ruhr, he has no profound sadness other than that for all people on both sides killed in the war. (As the late Group Captain Lord Cheshire wrote, just before he died: 'All Bomber Command regrets the fact that we had to be the ones to help prise open Fortress Europe in this way.')

Johnson also remembers that, at the time of Dresden, Germany was launching the V1 and V2 weapons indiscriminately against the UK and Belgium. His Lancaster was named *'Vergeltungswaffe'* (Vengeance Weapon) as a response to Germany's own

Vergeltungswaffen - the VIs and V2s.

Ken Redshaw does not believe that anyone could have foreseen loss of life due to lack of oxygen created by the firestorm. However, from the point of view of the RAF bomber crews, Dresden was as legitimate a target as were Manchester, Liverpool and Coventry to their German counterparts. Redshaw was still only twenty years old when he finished his tour of operations.

A Church of England padre, a Flight Lieutenant who wore the flying badge of an air-gunner, was asked to reconcile his brevet with his religious convictions, and he replied by saying that he had fought for his religion as well as for his country, and because Hitler and his gang had supressed religion.

A Halifax bomber navigator, who later became a Methodist minister, said that fighting Hitler was the lesser of two evils.

Leonard O'Hanlow firmly believes that the fight was for freedom from tyranny. Hitler's Germany was foul and evil, and had to be destroyed. For such tyranny to triumph was unthinkable: it had to be beaten at all costs.

Mr Gomersall[1], who was awarded the DFC, having taken into account the whole operation of the war in its broadest sense, and what he describes as his 'small contribution', has no sense of guilt about his involvement in the raid on Dresden. Having said that, he is also aware that war is a terrible business, but feels that WWII was necessary to defeat an even more terrible Nazi regime the like of which must never be allowed to rise again.

Peter Hoare had a pen-friend in Germany in the late

[1] - ***The term 'Mr' is applied throughout this chapter where individuals declined to use, or omitted, their service ranks and/or their forenames whilst in correspondence with the author.***

1930's - Gunter Heisig, who lived near Dresden and was a member of the Nazi Hitler Youth. He used to send Peter propaganda on the Third Reich, its aims and military strengths. Even at the age of fifteen it made Peter anxious.

Mr Nesbit feels that it was most unfortunate that so many women and children were victims, and that two wrongs don't make a right. Even when the Germans had known they were beaten they had started the V1 and V2 campaign without any regard to civilian casualties in the England and elsewhere in Europe. He feels that only God knows what would have happened if Germany had perfected the atomic bomb.

Bill Spence naturally regrets the loss of life and the destruction of a beautiful city, but remembers that this country was in a total war situation, and that civilians could not be differentiated from military personnel or military installations as they were very often in close proximity. There are regrets about any target which was attacked, but the raids were all part of a vital war effort to prevent evil ruling the world and, without attacks such as those Bomber Command carried out, the war would have been prolonged much longer. Spence feels that a wrong impression has been created that the only role Bomber Command carried out was saturation bombing of cities.

In 1988, Alan Russell, a New Zealander, saw a film about the bombing of Dresden which had been made by young people not even born when he was flying with Bomber Command. The film stressed the inhumane aspect of the bombing, saying that innocent civilians had been killed, as well as much of Germany's cultural centre having been destroyed. After it had been shown the owner of the film asked for comments. Russell spoke up quickly, saying:

> 'Before the war I worked for a big civil engineering firm employing perhaps 300 men. That firm had a motto:- "A good man does as he is told". He has to make the whole effective although, of course, he cannot be sure that the part he has been given to play is supporting the other parts of the endeavour.
> I was at that briefing and flew on that raid: we were not told anything about refugees or the cultural centre. We were shown recent photographs of the loaded marshalling railway yards, and the purple and black night-bombing map had shown that the yards were large enough to make a broad target. Ten-tenths cloud over the target did not help the accuracy of our bombing, but the marker flares assured that the bombing was concentrated.'

When Russell asked the owner of the film: 'If you had been assigned to that raid, would you have refused to go?' he would not answer. Russell continued:

> 'Remember, Germany was practising decimation of the Jews and other non-German races at that time, and had exterminated several million humans. All wars, unfortunately, overflow to civilians and even now I have no regrets about anything in which I was involved which was designed to slow down and finally stop the German war machine. "A good man does as he is told".'

Sid Baker's father was a policeman in London during the Blitz. On one occasion, he was the first on the scene of the bombing of a block of flats in Stoke Newington, North

London. About 300 people were killed in this bombing, and the horrible sights he saw remained with him until his death, just after the end of the war. Both he and his wife's family were bombed out of their home in London.

Robert Lythgoe maintains that if civilians are killed deliberately, a feeling of guilt exists for anyone who has a conscience. However, when the target is military first and foremost, and a large bomber force carries out the raid, civilian casualties are inevitable, albeit regrettably, through sheer accident.

Bob Ryett was a prisoner-of-war and saw the inhumane way the Nazis treated the Russians, Poles and other displaced people. He was of the opinion that the majority of the German race had collaborated with the Nazis.

Reg Small was another who lived in London during the war, and admits sorrow for the many thousands who perished that night in Dresden, but he wonders if the Germans have forgotten Warsaw, Rotterdam, Southampton, Coventry and London.

From Canada, Fraser Muir feels that it was too bad that the attack on Dresden had to take place. But, having said that, he has no remorse or feelings of guilt. The Germans, he feels, brought it on themselves, but it was sad that so many young men had to die to satisfy the desires of a madman, and of a nation which believed its people were born to rule the world.

On VE Day in 1945, Leslie Hay was on leave in his home town of Plymouth. He stood in the ruins and surveyed the devastation. A large area had been flattened, and was a mass of twisted girders and rubble. Streets along which he had walked on his way home from school were unrecognisable, and some had disappeared altogether. As he stood there, he reflected on the past six years and his raids on Germany, including Dresden. His heart went out to the French, Belgians and Dutch, men, women and children who had been killed resisting the enemy in their countries. For Dresden he sheds no tears.

Mr Reid has no regrets or guilt whatsoever. 'We were at war' he says, 'and considering what they had done to our cities, it was a case of "Take that".' An officer he knew in the Navy had his wife and two children killed in an air raid, and immediately remustered to aircrew in the RAF. Another trainee with Mr Reid also had his family killed in a raid.

Harold Whowell, having seen the blitz on Coventry, has no qualms about bombing Dresden, and quotes Edith Piaf: - 'No Regrets.'

Dennis Bolesworth feels no guilt at all about Dresden, but a little sadness about the porcelain connection. He has no doubt that the raid saved Russian lives and shortened the war by destroying the railway yards etc.

Freddie Hulance also thinks that the raid on Dresden shortened the war, and that the bombing in general saved many civilian lives. In 1992 he was in Canada and met a German lady who had lived in that country for twenty-five years. She had been in Dresden during the raid. She described it as a horrific experience, and alleged that Allied aircraft had strafed refugees leaving the city, on the morning after the raid, in low level attacks. Hulance found her intelligent and well educated, but indoctrinated by Nazi propaganda, and apparently unaware that Germany had still been bombing England at the time of the raid on Dresden. However, there was no animosity and she kissed him on her departure.

When Dennis Morrison joined the RAF, he knew that he would probably end up on heavy bombers and that, as a result of his efforts, many people, mostly civilians, would be killed or terribly disabled. He thought that if this would help to win the war against a ruthless enemy, it would be as justifiable as killing soldiers who, in the main, were as innocent as most civilians and often just as scared. They just happened to be the right age at the wrong time. He had experienced the full effects of the Blitz against London, and his parents were still being subjected to the V1 and V2 attacks. The real villains of Dresden, he feels, were the Nazis, aided by our own politicians, who let them get away with aggression until it was almost too late, and for four years relied on the bomber offensive as our only means of striking back at Germany.

In 1934/35, Ernest Millington was a pacifist taking part in the Peace Pledge campaign of that time. Hitler, he says, made him change his mind. The war had to be pursued as ruthlessly as possible, which meant killing the enemy and risking being killed himself. He not only became a bomber pilot, but also commanded a squadron and so had to send men out night after night, knowing exactly what they would face and, as a pilot, often going with them.

In 1991, Mr Buxton, who had been a navigator with 227 Squadron, visited Berlin with his local Rotary Club: whilst there, to his great dismay, a day trip to Dresden was arranged. He was almost tempted to pull out, as it was the last place in Germany he wanted to visit. However, he went, and heard the German hosts and guides make reference to the destruction and casualties: he found the day a most uncomfortable one. The city had been partially rebuilt with poor quality property which resembled, he felt, some council estates in the UK in the 1950/60's.

One ex-navigator firmly believes that the devastating destruction caused in Dresden was contributed to by exceptionally high winds. He also feels that it was a psychological blow to the Germans which resulted in the war ending many months earlier than it would otherwise have done and, in so doing, probably saved hundreds of thousands of lives at death camps, as well as those of Allied troops. He reminds us that the Germans were still operating concentration camps, and that many prisoners were being murdered every day.

'All war is Hell, and nobody in their right senses wants it,' says John de Bell Hurst, 'but there comes a time when it seems unavoidable without giving up your freedom and becoming slaves to the bully.' In war, young men are made to do terrible deeds that they would not dream of in peacetime. This has always been so, and Hurst supposes it always will be. The onus must rest with the country's leaders of the day.

Wing Commander Cox served with 214 Squadron and 7 (Pathfinder) Squadron, which he commanded. He went on to complete thirty-six years in the RAF, and feels that if it was wrong to bomb Dresden, then it was wrong to bomb all the other major towns in Germany. He feels sadness today for the 50,000 plus men of Bomber Command who 'bought it'.

For those who believe that the German Air Force was finished at the time of Dresden, Ron Durran, who flew on Lancasters with 576 Squadron, reminds them of the losses on operations after that raid. On 16th March 1945, over a month after Dresden, thirty aircraft were shot down, three from 576 Squadron, and his aircraft had half its port wing shot away. The nightfighters had pounced on the bomber force as it made its bombing run into Nuremberg.

Eric Wilkin's flight engineer from his first Pathfinder tour was killed while flying with another crew on 5th April 1945, seven weeks after Dresden. He reminds us that approximately 500,000 German civilians were killed in air raids during the war, for a cost of 56,000 aircrew of Bomber Command: this averages ten German civilians for every airman killed. But, he asks, how many German servicemen were killed when the Germans massacred six million people in concentration camps?

William Topper, who dropped the first marker on Dresden, reflects today that the UK was up against an evil movement which tried to engulf and suppress Western Europe. For the first three years of the war, Bomber Command was the only weapon able to strike far afield in Germany and Italy. It was an effort which had to be kept up to the end, neither stopped nor changed in direction until victory was assured. That could not happen until the enemy put down his weapons. Topper today is sad at the loss of life and beauty, but believes that greater losses might have been incurred if the task had not been carried on until the end was achieved.

Mr Tarry had seen the work of the *Luftwaffe* at close-hand, having been involved in fire-watching in London in 1940/42, and having served with 514 and 7 Squadrons.

Ron James was a bomb aimer: he says today that all bomb aimers were aware that civilians were being killed, and accepted that as the price of total warfare.

The German SS General Sepp Dietrich said that not even the best troops could stand bombing night and day. Rommel said: 'Stop the bombing, or we cannot win the war. All we get by going on is to lose another city each night.'

On 15th March 1945, Speer sent a message to Hitler: 'Owing to the utter dislocation of the German transport system German industry is bound to come to a standstill within eight weeks.'

Five days before the end of the war, in May 1945, Speer said on German radio: 'Repair of the German railway system is your most important task, or starvation faces us.'

On 2nd March 1945, Arthur Harris wrote to Eisenhower, expressing great concern about his Command and feelings towards it. He mentioned in this letter that

Bomber Command had virtually destroyed sixty-three leading industrial towns in Germany, and vastly damaged a great many more. His concern was the lack of credit given to the bomber forces, including the American 8th Air Force, by correspondents accompanying the armies as they advanced. He went on to mention the 'railway war' before D-Day. In particular, he referred to the German town of Aachen: the media despatches stated that all the industrial and other damage in the city was due to the effects of artillery bombardment and the tactical air force attacks. Aachen had in fact been severely damaged by Bomber Command in June 1944 when it destroyed the marshalling yards as part of the pre-invasion 'railway war'.

On 5th April 1945, a Minute was sent to the Prime Minister by the Secretary, Chiefs of Staff Committee on the subject of area bombing:-

(a) Area bombing designed solely with the object of destroying or disorganising industrial areas should be discontinued.

(b) There should be no alteration to the current bombing directive such as would exclude area bombing.

(c) Area attacks may prove necessary against those targets the destruction of which is calculated best to assist the advance of the Allied armies into Germany or to have the most immediate effect upon the enemy's ability to continue armed resistance.

(d) Any ultimate political or economic disadvantages of area bombing necessitated by those operations should be accepted.

On 19th April 1945, came a Directive from the Chiefs of Staff in which the overall mission of the strategic air forces was stated as :-

'The progressive destruction and dislocation of the German military, industrial and economic systems and the direct support of land and naval forces.'

The chief reasons were given as :-

(a) The extent to which the destruction and dislocation of enemy industrial and economic systems has already been achieved.

(b) The extensive advances of Allied armies into Germany.

(c) The need for avoiding unnecessary destruction of facilities which will be needed for our occupying forces.

Serious in-depth research over many years shows that, from February 1945, the German military, industrial and economic system collapsed rapidly.

In an official report from Munich dated March 1944:

'Morale has gone down to a level never experienced since war began. The terror due to air bombardment has proved so far the major important factor in the collapse of morale.'

Planned dates for the end of the war against Germany were drawn up, the earliest being 1st July 1945, and that beyond which the war was thought unlikely to continue being 31st December 1945. The war against Japan was estimated to end eighteen months after the defeat of Germany. It seems likely, therefore, that the intense raids on the eastern German cities, and certainly the dropping of the atomic bombs, accelerated progress towards the ending of the war.

CHAPTER FIFTEEN

POST WAR

After the cessation of hostilities, it was possible to begin to draw together evidence from numerous and diverse sources. From these, assessments could begin to be made about the effectiveness of the Allied bombing policy.

Between September 1939 and 2/3rd May 1945, the date of the last operation by Bomber Command, it had mounted 391,137 sorties against German targets, dropping 2.7 million tons of bombs, of which 657,674 tons were on Germany. It had also dropped 47,250 mines, sinking or damaging 1,000 ships, more than any other branch of the RAF or the Royal Navy.

The German Air Force had lost 19,923 bombers and 52,042 fighters, the RAF 22,000 aircraft and the US Air Force 18,000. The number of men lost on operations with Bomber Command was 47,293, of whom 35,637 were lost over Germany. On the Runnymede Memorial there are 20,435 names of men and women who have no known graves: many of them were from Bomber Command crews. The German Air Force lost 96,917 killed, wounded or missing.

In the 1914/18 war, approximately one airman was killed for every hundred soldiers. In WWII, the comparable figures were seventy airmen for every hundred soldiers.

The total German manpower affected by air-raid damage was estimated at between 1,000,000 and 1,500,000 people, as reported by Dr Speer in 1945. His statement said:

'There is no doubt that, in the absence of air raids, it would have been possible to withdraw several hundred thousand more soldiers from the armaments industry at the end of 1943. A large proportion of German skilled labour was required at the factories for bomb damage clearance, where their specialised knowledge and keenness to restore the plants made their presence indispensable after air attacks. If no air raids had taken place, we should have been able to increase the proportion of foreign and unskilled labour. Furthermore, during 1944, Army training units were increasingly employed on bomb damage clearance work, leading to a reduction in the standard of training and to a lengthening of training schedules.

The continuous bomber offensive kept a considerable amount of German armament production inside Germany, thus withholding it from the Front. Some 30% of the total output of guns in 1944 consisted of Anti-Aircraft (flak) guns, while some 20% of that year's output of the heavier calibres of ammunition, from 7cm upwards, consisted of Anti-Aircraft shells. Between 50% and 55% of the armaments production capacity of the electro-technical industry was engaged in the manufacture of radar and signals equipment for defence against bomber attacks. 33% of the optical industry was engaged in the production of aiming devices for Anti-Aircraft guns, and of other anti-aircraft equipment. The fighting power of the *Wehrmacht* was considerably weakened by reason of the above, since the production of valuable flak guns would have supplied troops with excellent anti-tank weapons[1], and the use of flak ammunition at the Front, in addition to other types, would have provided a very substantial increase in stocks. Both were used only to a small extent in the final battles. The radar equipment industry was unable to keep up with the requirements of the Army and Navy, either from the point of view of development or of production. The position was made even more grave by the fact that 50% of the valves produced for the *Luftwaffe's* requirement was diverted to home defence needs.'

The statement continued by saying that transport difficulties caused by Allied air attacks were decisive in causing the swift breakdown of the Ardennes offensive. From captured German documents at the end of the war proof was found that, after these attacks, the Germans were severely short of aircraft, guns, tanks, ammunition, locomotives, rolling stock, lorries and clothing.

Goebbels stated that 60,000 houses out of a total of 230,000 in Germany were destroyed by the bombing.

Von Runstedt, who was in command of the counter-offensive in the Ardennes, stated after the war that Allied bombers had encompassed his downfall and that of the Reich. He said:

'Air power was the first decisive factor in Germany's defeat; lack of petrol and oil the second; and the destruction of the railways the third.'

[1] - *The 88mm flak gun was used throughout the war as a very potent anti-tank gun at zero elevation. Having to concentrate these weapons for the defence of the Reich from aerial attack spared innumerable Allied tank crews.*

He went on to say:

> 'The tremendous Allied superiority in the air, which paralysed movement of German troops, and the destruction of industrial centres and the loss of Silesia prevented the production of arms and ammunition. The Allied heavy bomber attacks on the German Army considerably reduced its power to resist the Allied offensive. During the campaign in Normandy in 1944, the laying of a bomb carpet in front of the advancing Allied troops considerably facilitated the task of infantry and armour. The bombing of German positions on the coast also minimised artillery opposition to the landing fleets, and softened up the coastal defences.'

Göring attributed the Allied victory over Germany to two main factors: a successful invasion and, above all else, the irresistible superiority of the Allied Air Forces. He had said: 'We have a lot of planes but no petrol. That is the trouble.' Without the Allied Air Force, Göring claimed, it would have been possible to have brought up German reinforcements in Normandy and made full use of armoured units.

Field Marshal Kesselring gave three reasons why Germany was defeated: Allied strategic bombing behind the German lines; attacks by low-flying Allied aircraft; and terror raids against the German civilian population.

General Milch mentioned that the Allied Pathfinder technique and its ability to locate the target was a vast improvement upon the German system used against Britain. He also said that the catastrophe of the German Army was due to destruction of the railways and the lack of lorries and fuel. He praised the fire-raising technique, whose excellence could not be improved upon, although he felt that the American close formation day bombing was more effective that the RAF night attacks.

The Managing Director of the Rhinemetall Borsig Works, which had employed 17,000 workers in the Rath-Grafenberg-Exe-Debendorf area said: 'If the heavy bombing of the Ruhr had been delayed for another year, the Western wall would never have been pierced. Allied bombing reduced German steel production from 20 million tons a year to almost nothing between 1942 and 1945.' (This fact was disclosed by the German Steel Syndicate.)

Herr Fritz Knickenberg, Chief Inspector of the Hamm rail district, had supervised 4,000 railway men and 8,000 casual labourers employed on rail repairs:

'At first your bombers came as regularly as our trains. Later, in 1943, they were far more punctual than our railway services, although you must admit that the railway engineers put up a stiff fight.'

He thought it would take several months to reconstruct the German railway system, and believed that one-third of German rolling stock was damaged beyond repair in air-raids. Two million foreign labourers, who had been employed for filling bomb craters or repairing railway lines, would have to be replaced by German workers to continue the work.

At the Essen Krupps works, the bombing had reduced output of raw steel and finished products to nil by 11th March 1945: at best production only just managed to resume with about eight per cent of the pre-bombing output. The controller of the works, Professor Edouard Houdremont, who employed 50,000 men in the Essen district, said:

> 'It was not so much the complete destruction of the plant itself that reduced or stopped output,

> but the paralysing effect of bombing raids on the supply system that caused most damage to war production. I would classify the effect of air raids as follows:-
>
> a. Bombs destroying installations, workshops, machines and buildings.
>
> b. Bombs hitting power mains, water pipes, railway bridges and canal barges, thereby cutting off supplies of power and raw materials.
>
> c. Loss of production hours through alerts which lasted, of course, very much longer than the actual raids and meant a complete standstill for several hours whilst all personnel were marshalling into shelters.

He continued by saying that, looking at the shambles of Krupp's, works, it was beyond a shadow of a doubt that the bombing had reduced the war potential of Germany to such an extent that it had shortened the war by at least two years.

Dr Eberhard Letixerant, Chief Technical Director of a steel works in Bochum, said:

> 'In pre-bombing days we turned out 65,000 tons of steel per month. We employed 30,000 men. This was reduced because of the raids to 40,000 tons, although the average sank below 50 per cent owing to losses of man-hours through repair work. Raids in 1943 continued to reduce the output.'

Dr Fritz Beitter, Chairman of the Dorsig Works at Dusseldorf, described the raid on 2nd November 1944 as the 'funeral of the plant'.

The Mannesmann Roehrenwerke at Rath, Dusseldorf, had produced 15,000 tons of water and oil pipes, shell cases and flak gun barrels per month. The raid on 2nd November 1944 stopped all production for four weeks, after which output was restored, but to only 50%.

Dr Hermann Brandi, the steelworks manager at a plant in Duisberg said:

> 'We could not cope with the air bombardment for three reasons:-
>
> a. Because the supply lines became so restricted and were so often cut that we could neither get nor despatch our own products, nor could we obtain sufficient power, gas, and water.
>
> b. Because air raids shortened the number of available man hours, and the necessity to employ unskilled labour in skilled jobs to make up for the loss made continuation difficult.
>
> c. Material damage that caused widespread destruction and destroyed vital parts of the whole machinery.'

Hauptmann Zimmerman, Chief Air Raid Warden at the Port of Bremen, revealed that the considerable stores of food, petrol, spares, ammunition etc. destined for the Western Front had been burnt in the numerous air attacks even as far back as 18th May 1940. Supplies intended for the planned German invasion of Britain in the summer of 1940 were burnt in a lightning raid which put the supply organisation back several months. U-Boat warfare was severely handicapped through consistent bombing of the

Bremen assembly plants and the U-Boat pens. The men who constructed the U-Boat assembly plants said:

> 'If you had not bombed Bremen, Hamburg and Kiel, apart from other targets, we would have had so many U-Boats that Admiral Doenitz's threat of throwing a ring of steel around the British Isles would have been virtually possible, and we can assure you that your bombs saved the lives of thousands of seamen who would have been threatened by our rapidly progressing submarine production, which was hampered and eventually frustrated by your Air Force.'

After the raid on Pforzheim in 1945, it was reported that the town's morale had disappeared along with its buildings, and the people dreamed only of the evil of the war.

A Russian war correspondent said: 'You have to see the streets of Berlin to realise what Allied raids really meant.'

General Karl Koller, Chief of the General Staff, and Head of *Luftwaffe* Operations, when interrogated in 1945, said that Germany had lost the war because of failing to attain air supremacy. Everything else, he maintained, must take second place. The Air Force in Germany was low down in the list of priorities, after submarines, tanks and guns.

In 1967, Sir Robert Saundby, Deputy C in C Bomber Command said:

> 'What is a military target and how can it be defined? The man who loads or fires a field gun is a military target. So is the gun and the ammunition for it. So is the driver who

> transports ammunition from the base to the ammunition dump. Are the men who make the weapons in the factories not targets? Gas, water and electricity installations which keep the industries going, are these not targets?'

A former captain in the British Army, having read of a slur against the RAF by an American newspaper, and having been in Dresden post-war (1945/46), attached to the Soviet Commander-in-Chief for Saxony, firmly believes that attacks such as that on Dresden were instrumental in the German withdrawal, and in speeding the Soviet advance. The aim was to bring the war to an end as soon as possible and, in so doing, save as many Allied lives as possible: without these attacks casualties would have been far greater than those suffered at Dresden.

In 1945, there were 190,256 officers and 1,006,267 airmen in the RAF, of whom the great majority were volunteers, serving in a vast number of trades and branches, many of which had been created during the war. It was the third largest Air Force in the world, only the American and Russian counterparts being larger. The bomber offensive cost only 7% of National Resources, but was 70% responsible for ending of the war.

There were some appreciative letters for the work and help of Bomber Command in the war. Field Marshal Bernard Montgomery, writing to Harris, said:

> 'Again, the Allied armies in France would like to thank you personally, and Bomber Command, for your magnificent co-operation. We know well that your main work lies further afield and we applaud your continuous and sustained bombing of German industries and the effect this has had on the German war effort. But we also

> know well that you are always ready to bring your mighty effort closer when such action is really needed, and to co-operate in our tactical battle. When you do this your action is always decisive.'

This message came after the attack on Caen in 1944. In 1945, after the crossing of the Rhine, he sent another message in which he thanked Bomber Command for its attack on Wesel, and went on to say how Fighter and Bomber Commands had beaten off the attacks on the UK in 1940 and shattered German invasion plans. He said the effect of air bombing was decisive and the spectacle terrific. 'The first of the three unchanging principles of modern warfare is - before you can attack on land, you must win the battle of the air.'

Stalin said, in March 1945:

> 'I welcome the bombing of Essen, Berlin and other industrial centres of Germany. Every blow delivered by your Air Force to the vital German centres evokes a most lively echo in the hearts of many millions throughout the length and breadth of our country.'

On 7th December 1944, Germany's 8th Abteilung Staff Study of the Allied Air Offensive on German Economic Life stated:

> 'The air war waged by the Allies until now against German territory has shown that a powerful Air Force can effectively dislocate the economic life of a nation possessing a numerically inferior Air Force. Prolonged attacks of growing intensity on bottle-neck industries

> and communications may well decide the outcome of a war.'

Extracts from *'The Rise and Fall of German War Economy, 1939-45,'* by Dr Wagenfuehr, war-time Head of the Statistical Department of the Planning Division of the Ministry of Armament and War Production, dated 30th July 1945:-

> 'During the Summer of 1944, a new and decisive strain was added to the many difficulties of German economy, - the systematic air attacks directed against communications and industrial plants ... The incredible intensification of aerial warfare is best expressed in the tonnage of bombs dropped on Germany, (mines, HE and incendiaries): in 1943, the figure was approximately 150,000 tons; in 1944, the total was between 550,000 and 600,000 tons, of which almost two-thirds were dropped in the second half of the year. Air attacks in March 1944 reduced industrial output by 30%, and in October by 60%.'

Jodl said of the effects on the German serviceman's morale:-

> 'The psychological effect of the bombing of German cities on the front-line soldier was very great. That is something that is frequently overlooked, but it was of the first importance in my opinion. While previously the soldier believed that by fighting at the Front he was protecting his native land, his wife and his children, this factor was completely eliminated and replaced by the realisation, "I may hold on

as much as I please, but still my wife and children go to the dogs".'

On 9th May 1945, a telegram was sent to Sir Arthur Harris by the Air Council:

> 'On this momentous occasion, the Air Council send their warmest congratulations and thanks to the men and women of Bomber Command for their superb contribution to the cause of the United Nations. For five long years, without halt or respite, the Command has carried the war to the heart of Germany. It has fought and won a series of mighty battles. It has brought destruction on an unparalleled scale to the *Wehrmacht* and its supporting industries, and played a decisive part in the final victory.
> The vision with which the Command's operations have been planned and executed against targets in land and sea, the ardour and skill with which its equipment has been developed and maintained and the matchless courage and determination with which its attacks have been pressed home have been beyond all praise.
> Our heartfelt thanks to you all.'

This was followed, on 15th May 1945, by a message to the C in C Bomber Command by Winston Churchill:

> 'Now that Nazi Germany is defeated, I wish to express to you all, on behalf of His Majesty's Government, the deep sense of gratitude which is felt by all the Nations for the glorious part which has been played by Bomber Command in forging the Victory. For over two years, Bomber Command alone carried the War to the heart of

Germany, bringing hope to the peoples of Occupied Europe and, to the enemy, a foretaste of the mighty power which was rising against him. As the Command expanded, in partnership with the Air Forces of our American Allies, the weight of the attack was increased, bringing destruction on an unparalleled scale to the Germany military, industrial and economic system. Your Command also gave powerful support to the Allied Armies in Europe, and made a vital contribution to the war at sea. You destroyed or damaged many of the enemy's ships at war and much of his U-Boat organisation. By prolonged series of mining operations, you sank or damaged large quantities of his merchant shipping. All your operations were planned with great care and skill; they were executed in the face of desperate opposition and appalling hazards. They made a decisive contribution to Germany's defeat. The conduct of these operations demonstrated the fiery, gallant spirit which animated your aircrews and the high sense of duty of all ranks under your command. I believe that the massive achievement of Bomber Command will long be remembered as an example of duty nobly done.'

Harris responded on 16th May 1945, thanking the Prime Minister and ending his reply by saying:

'To us you were foremost of the Pathfinders.'

However, for Harris and Bomber Command at the end of the war, there was little other praise. He left to live in South Africa, but before he left he had lunch with Churchill and General Alanbrooke. During the meal

Churchill became very angry, saying: 'Why were you left out of the Honours List?! I'll take it up with Attlee and remind him we were all in this.' Harris replied that he had been offered the alternatives of a promotion to the top rank of the RAF or a Peerage, and that he would rather have the rank and remain in respectable company! Churchill then said: 'You fought a thousand major battles and won most of them, a record unapproached in history. Jellicoe fought one, lost it, and they made him an Earl. They do things differently in and for the Navy!'

To be fair to Churchill, he was as good as his word and did write to Attlee to ask why Harris was not in the Honours List, mentioning the efforts of Bomber Command in shortening the war before the enemy could use their long-range weapons. He ended by saying that he hoped the omission could be rectified before Harris left for South Africa. The reply from Attlee was, to say the least, feeble: he said that promotion to Marshal of the RAF was what he felt adequate, and held out no hopes of revising the List.

Why did Churchill let Bomber Command down after the Dresden raid? Perhaps we shall never know, but one thing is sure. By trying to obtain an honour for Harris, he clearly regretted his lack of support for the attacks which he had advocated as early as 1940.

What was it like to serve under Harris? Many who did so never even saw him. But, with only seven days in a week and twenty-four hours in a day, it was impossible for him to be everywhere. On two of those seven days he was in London, trying, among other things, to secure better pay for the captains of his bombers, saying that the man sweeping the streets outside the Treasury got more than the men flying. He attempted also to obtain better equipment - in particular, better guns for the bombers, to put them on equal terms with the German fighters: they were using cannon while the bombers were still only armed with .303 Browning machine guns. He was frustrated by the war, and wanted to get it over as quickly as possible in order to save lives. He was known to his contemporaries as Bert as, at Staff College, all men with the name Harris were known. The country called him 'Bomber', the name Churchill had given him, and his crews called him 'Butch'. He did not mind in the least what his 'old lags' called him: he knew what they had given and the courage they had shown.

There are two clear examples of how anxious Harris was to end the war, relating to little-known incidents in WWII:

On 21st February 1941, before he had taken over as C in C Bomber Command, Harris wrote to Air Marshal Sholto Douglas at Fighter Command. He reminded him of the conversation they had had on 6th February about Hitler's pilot, a man called Hans Bauer, who had been commended for his devoted service. His father-in-law, a man named Kiroff, had approached the British Embassy in Sofia in December 1940, and had stated that Bauer, who was of Austrian extraction, and had lost two brothers flying in the war, had become disillusioned by the war: he was flying nearly every day as Hitler's pilot, and was apparently prepared to make a 'forced landing' in England with the *Führer* and members of his staff. The plan was to get Bauer's family out of Germany and into Belgrade before Bauer made the flight.

The simple instructions to Bauer were :

> I. Aircraft must approach the coastline and make a steep descent to Lympne aerodrome with its wheels down. The exact position seven miles due west of Folkestone.

2. Pilot to fire not less than four red flares at thirty second intervals if approached by British fighters.

3. As soon as aircraft lands, engines should be stopped and put out of action.

The last information known about Hitler's aircraft was that it was a four-engined Focke Wulf Condor. It was also known that Hitler flew over foreign territory twice a month, and was never without one or more of his senior staff. On the 26th, Douglas wrote to Air Vice Marshal Leigh-Mallory, outlining the possibility of a German deserter landing at Lympne, in Kent, by daylight. Various arrangements were made for anti-aircraft defences to be installed at Lympne, and seven officers and 150 soldiers of the Buffs Regiment were posted to the airfield.

On 7th March, a letter said that Kiroff had been to Vienna to meet Bauer, and had handed him the instructions, which he understood perfectly. Bauer had said that his aircraft was always escorted by three other aircraft, which flew at a considerable distance from the Condor, and for this reason he did not want flares fired. His plan was to drop, over Lympne, a number of small yellow metal plaques bearing the initials A.B. He also asked for a red light to be shown on the aerodrome. The most likely time was to be 25th March, or soon thereafter, between 5am and 6am or 6pm and 8pm.

The plan was to get Bauer's passengers away from the airfield as quickly as possible and take them straight to the Air Ministry by car under armed escort. A Ford V8 box-body touring car with driver and two motor-cycle outriders were laid on.

However, Harris's plan to abduct Hitler fell through when a message on 17th May 1941 said the 'special arrangements' which were about to be implemented were to be postponed for another two weeks. On 28th May 1941, the 'arrangements' were called off. Apparently Bauer had got cold feet.

On 3rd December 1942, Harris, now C in C Bomber Command, issued Operation Order No 162. A successful bombing attack directed against the buildings in which Mussolini worked and slept would have a profound effect on Italian public opinion.

Il Duce spent the night at the Villa Torlonia, and usually rose at 7am: his movements were known throughout the day, and the aim was to destroy the Palazzo Venezia, in which he had an office, and the Villa Torlonia in Rome, where he lived.

A force of twelve Lancasters of 5 Group was to carry out the attacks. No alternative targets were to be attacked, and the operation was to be carried out from very low level. The targets were to be attacked at 9.30am.

As before, for reasons unknown, the plan fell through. On 11th July 1943, Harris wrote to Portal, pointing out that permission had not been given to carry out the attack, and renewing his request to go ahead, this time using his 'old squadron' (as he called 617) who had, only two months earlier, so successfully attacked the Ruhr Dams in Germany. They would fly across France under cover of darkness, reach the targets at 9.30am and then go on to land in North Africa.

On the 13th, Portal wrote to Churchill, outlining Harris's plan. He pointed out that the targets were only 1,500 yards from the Vatican City, and said that, if Mussolini were to be killed or even badly shaken, it might greatly increase the chance of knocking Italy out of the war at an early date: he asked Churchill for permission to carry out the attack as soon as possible.

On the 14th, Anthony Eden wrote to Churchill, saying that he did not like the plan, and that he felt the chances of killing the Italian dictator were slight: Churchill replied on the 16th that he agreed with Eden.

These two examples show how Harris tried (albeit unsuccessfully) to shorten the war against Germany and Italy by taking the two dictators out of circulation.

Harris also tried very hard to secure a special medal for the bomber crews. Until June 6th 1944, a medal had been awarded (the Aircrew Europe Star), but thereafter it was discontinued. Those who took part in the Invasion and fought in Europe until the end of the war received the France and Germany Star. Even a Bar to this medal, with the inscription 'Bomber Command', would have sufficed, but it was not forthcoming.

The committee convened in 1946 to deal with the award of medals for WWII had only one RAF representative, and it is obvious from the Minutes of its meetings that it knew little about decorations, and how they should be awarded. To be fair, however, some pressure was put on the committee to decide as quickly as possible what medals should be awarded: had more time and thought been devoted to the subject, a more equitable conclusion might well have been reached.

Harris quoted the fact that, at Zeebrugge, in WWI, eight Victoria Crosses had been awarded, as well as 560 other decorations, whereas the men of Bomber Command were refused even a campaign medal.

On 27th December 1953, Field Marshal Montgomery said:

> 'First of all you must win the battle of the air. This must come before you start a single sea or land engagement. If you examine the course of my campaign you will find that we never fought a land battle until the air battle had been won.'

In 1960, Clement Attlee, the wartime Deputy Prime Minister and first post-war Prime Minister, said that he thought Harris 'was never frightfully good' and insisted that attacks on cities did not pay as much as more effective use of bombs on 'military targets.' Harris replied that targets and strategy were decided by the Government of the time, of which Attlee had been a prominent member, and that the decision to bomb industrial cities for 'morale effect' had been made, and was in force, before he became C-in-C Bomber Command.

In December 1940, Harris had stood on the roof of the Air Ministry and watched London on fire: he had seen at least eight Wren churches burning. He had been so incensed that he had sent for Charles Portal, Chief of the Air Staff, to see what the German bombing had done, and had then said: 'They have sown the wind' [... but they shall reap the whirlwind]. They had indeed, from Dresden to Hiroshima, where 85,000 were killed, and Nagasaki where 35,000 lost their lives, in the atomic bomb attacks.

In the recent Gulf War, the rate of air raids was four times higher than that of the 1939/45 war, so that form of warfare which was started in 1915 by the Zeppelin attacks still, sadly, continues today. As I write the last words of this book, NATO has been forced to use the formidable air power at its disposal to stop the Serb shelling of Sarejavo.

In 1990, Jimmy Hughes of the Pathfinder Association wrote:

> 'In 1945, with the end of the war, hypocritical and inept politicians did not want to know of the bombing raids. Rather like Pontius Pilate, they did the ritual washing of their hands over the whole affair.'

In 1981, a young Irish composer wrote a *Requiem* for the bombing of Dresden. When friends of his in Dresden heard it, they said that he should first have it played in Coventry: this was done and later, on 13th February 1985, the *Requiem* was performed in Dresden, on the 40th anniversary of the raid.

In 1980, Albert Speer, when interviewed by the author at his home in Heidelberg, said that criticism of Harris was unfounded, and that he (Speer) had, in fact, been surprised that more attacks had not been conducted on the lines of that on Hamburg. He also said that, as well as attacking cities, Bomber Command had also had its precision targets. He went on to say that, although German production had not ceased altogether, it had been severely curtailed, and the figures he had set were not reached: 30% of estimated production had been lost due to bombing. The bombing of Berlin, Speer said, had contributed to the downfall of Germany: he was astonished that all the Allies' books on WWII seemed to have overlooked the fact that the bombing of Germany had actually brought about its defeat.

A German navigator once calculated: 'Every time I fly, a million people take to their shelters.' Nevertheless, in London, morale rallied after the initial shock, and despite the fact that the capital was targeted for seventy-six consecutive nights, the intensity of the raids was gradually diluted as bombers were tasked against other cities.

Plans to erect a statue to the late C in C Bomber Command, Sir Arthur Harris, in 1992, caused renewed debate about the bombing of Dresden and Cologne. Protests came from the Mayor of Dresden, Herr Herbert Wagner, and the Mayor of Cologne, Norbert Burger, who made a statement explaining why he felt such statues should not be put up - referring not only to Harris but to all war heroes of the past. Herr Burger said:

> 'I do not want to hurt anybody's feelings in England. There is no doubt that anyone can put up a statue for any person. But I take the right to

> have my own thoughts about it - and say so. Especially when - like the people of Cologne - we are concerned.
> Firstly, I want to clear up any misunderstandings: I know Hitler started the war - Germany is responsible for it. I also know: the Germans were the first who planned and carried out carpet bombing against civilians: in Guernica, Warsaw, Rotterdam, Belgrade, London and Coventry. Hitler committed suicide: other Nazi leaders were justly tried as war criminals and hanged. I am also quite aware of the fact that Hitler's terrible crimes against the Jews and other minorities will remain unprecedented. The Holocaust is the darkest chapter of German History.'

Most British newspapers took the view at the time of these protests that the memorial was intended to honour our heroes, and not to glorify war. One stated that, had it not been for the boys of Bomber Command and thousands more British servicemen like them, Europe would not exist, and the only statue in the Strand would be of Adolf Hitler.

The late Lord Cheshire, a retired Group Captain in the RAF and holder of the Victoria Cross, said that the decision to bomb Dresden was a political one made by the War Cabinet and backed by the Americans. Without it, he said, there would have been no re-entry into Europe in 1944. Mistakes were made but made in good faith at the time, fifty years ago.

Sir Michael Beetham, a Marshal of the Royal Air Force, former Chief of the Air Staff and wartime bomber pilot, and now the President of the Bomber Command Association, said that a statue to Harris and his men was the very least they deserved.

The statue of Sir Arthur Harris.
The inscription at the base reads:

MARSHAL OF THE ROYAL AIR FORCE
SIR ARTHUR HARRIS BT GCB OBE AFC

IN MEMORY OF A GREAT COMMANDER AND
OF THE BRAVE CREWS OF BOMBER COMMAND.
MORE THAN 55,000 OF WHOM LOST THEIR
LIVES IN THE CAUSE OF FREEDOM.

THE NATION OWES THEM ALL AN IMMENSE DEBT.

There was talk at the time of the Queen Mother not unveiling the statue because of the controversy, and because of a report that a former navigator in Bomber Command had written to say how ashamed he was about having been part of the bombing campaign. However, this turned out to be totally untrue and, on 31st May 1992, outside St Clement Danes, the RAF Church in the Strand, London, the statue was unveiled. Apart from a few outbursts during the ceremony, the occasion went very well: however, only days after the unveiling, the statue was covered in red paint, and the word 'Shame' daubed on it.

In 1995, a Dresden Trust was set up to rebuild the *Frauenkirche*, a baroque church in Dresden, as a memorial to victims of aerial bombardment everywhere.

The Director of International Ministry at Coventry Cathedral, the Reverend Canon Paul Oestreicher, said that a substantial contribution had been made to Coventry Cathedral. The windows of the Cathedral's Chapel of Unity were paid for through an appeal for Coventry by the German Protestant Church. The ruined vestries of the destroyed Cathedral were restored and rebuilt with help from young German volunteers. Also, young people from Britain went to Dresden and helped to rebuild the Deaconess, destroyed in 1945. A bell, known as the Coventry Bell, was presented by the President of Germany on the 50th Anniversary of the destruction of Coventry Cathedral, and is rung each day before midday prayers.

In 1945, General Koller said:

'We have been beaten and eliminated. It will be interesting to watch the development of the Great Powers and the battle of wits. Will it be as it always has been, that they all, every one of them, will not learn from the past, and will continue to make the old mistakes again and again?'

Speer said:

> 'The possibility of the repetition of absolute rule by one man, surrounded by weaklings, must be prevented for all time to come. On this question there should not even be the opportunity of a free choice. Never again must the path of a nation be allowed to depend so exclusively on one pair of eyes; or be determined to such an extent by the mind and the abilities of a single man, as was the case in the era of Adolf Hitler.'

As far as Hitler was concerned, he had no remorse or regrets. In his last political testament, dated 29th April 1945, time 4pm, place Berlin, he wrote: 'Above all, I enjoin the government of the nation and the people to uphold the racial laws to the limit and to resist mercilessly the poisoner of all nations, international Jewry.' Two of the witnesses were Dr Joseph Goebbels and Martin Bormann.

In Dresden, the schoolchildren are taught that the raid was the result of Hitler's fanaticism.

His Majesty King George the Sixth said:

> 'In defending ourselves we were defending the liberties of the whole World.'

CHAPTER SIXTEEN

CONCLUSIONS

In conclusion we have to ask, was Dresden a legitimate military target? Sir Arthur Harris wrote, in a footnote to his letter of 29th March to Norman Bottomley (see page 194):

> 'Actually Dresden was a mass of munitions works, an intact government centre, and a key transportation point to the east. It is now none of these things.'

It is surely fair to assume that Harris had access to the latest intelligence information before the raid, and to the analysis of both intelligence and photographic evidence afterwards. Certainly, throughout his career, he was not known to be given to using unsubstantiated information; in fact, quite the reverse.

Colonel Harold E. Cook of the USAAF wrote, in a letter published in 'The Vancouver Sun':

> 'In 1944 at age 19 I had flown 38 missions out of Africa and Italy with both RAF and USAAF. I was shot down over Austria on May 24, 1944 and four of my crew were killed. On or about Jan. 30, 1945 we were evacuated from Stalag-Luft III in Silesia because of the advance of the Soviet Army, marched several days in sub-zero weather and then loaded onto German freight cars - 60 men where 40 would have been crowded. The night before the RAF/USAAF raids on Feb. 13/14, we were shunted into the Dresden marshalling yard where for nearly 12

> hours German troops and equipment rolled into and out of Dresden. I saw with my own eyes that Dresden was an armed camp: thousands of German troops, tanks and artillery and miles of freight cars loaded with supplies supporting and transporting German logistics towards the East to meet the Russians.'

A post-war report states:

> 'In order to do justice to the men who not only planned but executed the raids on Dresden, which took place in February, 1945, it is essential to place the attacks in the context of contemporary events. A bare six weeks earlier von Rundstedt's offensive in the Ardennes had proved that in spite of the war on two fronts and the intensive strategic bombing to which Germany had been subjected, the country's military strength was still most formidable. In Allied Headquarters, in January, 1945, a mood of extreme caution, even of pessimism, replaced the easy optimism of early December, 1944. It seemed that the war might drag on for at least another year. Germany still controlled extensive areas of Europe. In spite of the bombing, the production of weapons was considerable. Allied air supremacy was threatened by the increasing production of jet fighters. The schnorkel submarine had introduced a new factor into naval warfare. The impressive figure of another 23 divisions had been added to the strength of the German army and a people's force to defend the Reich was already in being...

And continues:

> 'At the Yalta Conference between Stalin, Churchill and Roosevelt on 4 February, 1945, General Antonov, the Deputy Chief of Staff of the Red Army, asked that the Germans should be prevented from moving troops to the East from the Western Front, Norway and Italy 'by air attacks against communications', specific mentions being made of Leipzig and Berlin. In broad request such as this made by the Russians for the bombing of communications targets, Dresden did not need to be expressly included. The city was a vital link in the reinforcement route to the Eastern Front, being at the centre of an extensive transportation system reaching out to Berlin, Vienna, Chemnitz, Leipzig, Breslau and Prague. It had long been on the official list of targets drawn up by the Ministry of Economic Warfare. Besides being the capital of Saxony and made all the more important as an administrative centre by the heavy bombing of Berlin, it included some thirty objectives of strategic importance including engineering works, factories making small arms and gun components, electrical motors, precision and optical instruments and chemicals. The city's own population of 600,000 had been considerably augmented by an influx of refugees from Berlin (the US Air Force had launched a particularly devastating daylight attack on Berlin on 3 February) and from the Russian advance.'

And concludes overleaf:

'It is difficult, even in the light of post-war research, to assess accurately the efforts (sic) of the Dresden raids, particularly as the city is in the eastern zone of Germany and many relevant records have not been accessible. However, it can be fairly said that from this month, February, 1945, dates the rapidly accelerating collapse of Germany's military, industrial and economic system. However, as a well-informed senior Luftwaffe Officer stated at the end of the war, "Pressure by the Gestapo succeeded for a long time in maintaining an artificial morale, in spite of intense bombardment, but that a limit to this could be reached is clearly exemplified in the case of Dresden. When this catastrophe became known to the whole of Germany, morale disintegrated everywhere in spite of the best or worst efforts of the Gestapo."'

One of the crews: Standing left to right:- F/Sgt Jack Ross (Flight Engineer); F/Sgt Ian Henderson (Navigator); (sitting) Flt/Lt Don Legg (South African - Captain); F/Sgt Andy Ross (Mid-upper Gunner); F/Sgt Russ Rawlings (Canadian - W/Operator); F/O Dave Jones (Bomb Aimer); (squatting) F/Sgt Jock Beat (Rear Gunner). Those without Mae Wests (life jackets) were the ground crew whose names, unfortunately, are not, recorded.

What of the airmen? Those men to whose sacrifices and undoubted courage the politicians refused to attribute any tangible recognition. Do they deserve to be branded as *'Terrorflieger'* or *'Luftganster'* by 'friend' and former foe alike? Nöel Coward penned the poem overleaf on that subject:

LIE IN THE DARK AND LISTEN

Lie in the dark and listen,
It's clear tonight so they're flying high
Hundreds of them, thousands perhaps,
Riding the icy, moonlight sky.
Men, materials, bombs and maps
Altimeters and guns and charts
Coffee, sandwiches, fleece-lined boots
Bones and muscles and minds and hearts
English saplings with English roots
Deep in the earth they've left below.
Lie in the dark and let them go
Lie in the dark and listen.

Lie in the dark and listen
They're going over in waves and waves
High above villages, hills and streams,
Country churches and little graves
And little citizen's worried dreams.
Very soon they'll have reached the sea
And far below them will lie the bays
And coves and sands where they used to be
Taken for summer holidays.
Lie in the dark and let them go
Lie in the dark and listen.

Lie in the dark and listen
City magnates and steel contractors,
Factory workers and politicians
Soft, hysterical little actors
Ballet dancers, 'Reserved' musicians,
Safe in your warm, civilian beds.
Count your profits and count your sheep
Life is flying above your heads
Just turn over and go to sleep.
Lie in the dark and let them go
Theirs is a world you'll never know
Lie in the dark and listen.

Lastly, a thought from a military man who agonized over the involvement of civilians in warfare:

'War is cruelty... and all those who brought War deserve all the curses and maledictions a people can pour out.'

General William Tecumseh Sherman (1820- 1891)
Union Army 1861 - 1865

APPENDIX ONE

AIRCRAFT LOSSES

1945

January	132
February	178
March	223
April	72
May	3
TOTAL	**608**

APPENDIX TWO

BOMBER COMMAND

AIRCREW LOSSES

RAF	
KILLED ON OPERATIONS	32,582
FLYING ACCIDENTS	5,669
RCAF	
KILLED ON OPERATIONS	8,048
FLYING ACCIDENTS	1,662
RAAF	
KILLED ON OPERATIONS	3,412
FLYING ACCIDENTS	627
RNAF	
KILLED ON OPERATIONS	1,416
FLYING ACCIDENTS	235

SAAF	
KILLED ON OPERATIONS	30
FLYING ACCIDENTS	10
INDIAN AIR FORCE	
KILLED ON OPERATIONS	6
FLYING ACCIDENTS	2
EGYPTION AIR FORCE	
KILLED ON OPERATIONS	1
FLYING ACCIDENTS	1
ALLIED	
KILLED ON OPERATIONS	1,110
FLYING ACCIDENTS	268
TOTAL KILLED ON OPERATIONS AND IN ACCIDENTS	**56,424**

AIRCREW

LOSSES BY CATEGORY

ON OPERATIONS

Pilots	5,957
Flight Engineers	4,357
Navigators	2,920
Wireless Operators	6,819
Bomb Aimers	2,415
Air Gunners	7,764

IN FLYING ACCIDENTS

Pilots	1,474
Flight Engineers	428
Navigators	485
Wireless Operators	1,270
Bomb Aimers	418
Air Gunners	908